Circle
Time

AGES 5–11

Jenny Mosley and Pat Child

Author
Jenny Mosley and Pat Child

Editor
Sally Gray

Assistant Editor
Catherine Gilhooly

Project Editor
Wendy Tse

Series designer
Joy Monkhouse

Designers
Erik Ivens
Melissa Leeke

Illustrations
DUNK

Cover photographs
© Scholastic Ltd

Published by Scholastic Ltd,
Villiers House,
Clarendon Avenue,
Leamington Spa,
Warwickshire
CV32 5PR

Printed by Bell & Bain Ltd, Glasgow
Text © 2005 Jenny Mosley and Pat Child
© 2005 Scholastic Ltd
    4 5 6 7 8 9 0   7 8 9 0 1 2 3 4

Visit our website at www.scholastic.co.uk

British Library Cataloguing-in-Publication Data
A catalogue record for this book is available from
the British Library.

ISBN 0-439-96511-X
ISBN 978-0439-96511-8

Material from the National Curriculum
© The Queen's Printer and Controller of
HMSO. Reproduced under the terms of
HMSO Guidance Note 8.
Material from the NLS © Crown Copyright.
Reproduced under the terms of HMSO
Guidance Note 8.

Every effort has been made to trace
copyright holders and the publisher
apologises for any inadvertent omissions.

Due to the nature of the web, the publisher
cannot guarantee the content or links of
any of the websites referred to. It is the
responsibility of the reader to assess the
suitability of websites.

Contents

Chapter 3 – Keeping healthy

Chapter 4 – Developing good relationships

Introduction

The Quality Circle Time model has been developed over the last 20 years by Jenny Mosley and has many key features that make it exceptionally useful to classroom teachers when they decide how best to deliver the curriculum for personal, social, emotional and citizenship education. All the activities in this *New Bright Ideas: Circle Time* book, follow this model and practitioners can be sure that by following the step-by-step circle time plans in this book they will be delivering exciting, inspiring, reassuring and high quality circle time experiences for the children in their care.

The ethos of circle time

Each circle meeting comprises a range of activities that are connected by a chosen theme. It is vital to start with an energetic, entertaining and inclusive opening that creates an atmosphere of fun and emotional safety. After establishing a warm, relaxed ethos you are then able to move sensitively into opening up important issues that concern your children. This is followed by more activities to help calm the children and leave them feeling emotionally strengthened and refreshed.

Circle meetings are innately democratic and non-competitive. A wide variety of teaching methods are employed to ensure that all children can use their particular abilities and aptitudes at some point in the proceedings. The brisk pace of the activities means that no one gets the chance to feel bored or lose interest in the lesson. Circle time should be timetabled at least once a week for 30–45 minutes. Younger children may respond to having shorter, more frequent circle meetings.

Planning and managing effective circle times

Children's emotional health is of crucial importance, so it is vital that you choose a time when everyone is feeling upbeat and energetic. Circle time is not something that you should do to wile away a Friday afternoon when everyone is tired and grouchy. Before you begin, you will need to make sure that you have sufficient space for all of your children to sit in the circle and engage in the activities that happen inside it. Make sure that this space is cleared of anything that may distract the children.

Short circle meetings can be held on the carpet, but the longer circle meetings are better held on chairs. This helps you to teach positive body language. Ground rules help meetings run smoothly and these can be agreed during the first session. You will need to work on these with everyone and then remind everyone at the beginning of each meeting. It is best to put them up on the wall for easy reference during your sessions. Ensure that adult helpers and visitors keep the rules alongside the children. The ground rules listed on page 6 have proved very successful.

Circle time ground rules

● We are here to boost up not to 'put down'.

It is vital that a positive atmosphere is maintained throughout the meeting. There must be no naming of anyone in a negative way because each session is about teaching and reinforcing healthy, respectful behaviours.

● We pay attention and listen carefully.

One of the great strengths of circle time is that it gives children the opportunity to discover that they have great wisdom and life experience to share with one another. Attentive listening is the key to productive circle meetings. Initially, you may find that you need to remind your class quite frequently (and politely!) that they must show each other respect by listening carefully and thinking about other people's opinions and viewpoints.

● We will not interrupt.

● We will put up our hands or use the 'speaking object' when we wish to speak.

● We have the right to say 'pass'.

Circle meetings are democratic, so every child has the right to speak but also the right to remain silent. Clearly, you will be there to encourage them if they are shy or hesitant, but it is important that they know they can say, 'pass' if they so wish. Encourage shy children to speak up by acquainting them, in a small circle at a different time of the week, with what is going to happen in the big class circle.

Giving praise

To maintain the positive ethos that is at the heart of every circle meeting you need to give regular praise and recognition to children who show evidence of good social skills. It is vital that you do not neglect children who are always well-behaved and respectful to others. Keep a little notebook entitled 'Points to praise' to ensure that praise is distributed fairly.

Using this book

The meetings described in this book are designed to address issues covered by PSHE and citizenship at Key Stages 1 and 2. Each session begins with a statement of its learning objectives and curriculum links, followed by a step-by-step explanation of the session. Each plan includes examples of questions that you may want to ask the children as well as the points that you will need to look out for as the meeting progresses. You will quickly find that you gain confidence and will soon feel that you can add touches of spontaneity and imagination that could help your meetings meet the specific needs and strengths of your particular class; but it is important to follow the plans carefully when you first begin using circle time.

Glossary

A 'speaking object' is used in the sessions to show whose turn it is to speak. When someone is holding the 'speaking object', they have the right to speak uninterrupted. It can then be passed to the next person. Use a small object, which children can hold easily in their hand. Decorated wooden eggs are ideal.

A round is used during the sessions to remind every child that they have a right to speak and to be heard. 'A round' usually involves the teacher giving the group the beginning of a sentence, such as, *My favourite game is… .* This passes around the circle – each child repeats the words and completes the sentence as they choose.

Further information

Jenny Mosley Consultancies provide training for schools in all aspects of circle time. Visit the website www.circle-time.co.uk or call 01225 767157 for more information.

CHAPTER 1

Developing confidence and responsibility

AGE RANGE 5–7

LEARNING OBJECTIVE
To recognise what they like and dislike.

CURRICULUM LINKS
QCA citizenship: Unit 1 – Taking part; Unit 2 – Choices.
KS1: En1 Speaking and listening (3) Group discussion and interaction.

Likes and dislikes

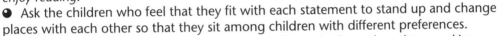

What you need
A 'speaking object' (see the introduction on page 6); photocopiable page 23.

What to do

Introductory phase
● Call out different likes and dislikes such as: *children who like sausages; children who dislike broccoli; children who like swimming; children who enjoy reading.*
● Ask the children who feel that they fit with each statement to stand up and change places with each other so that they sit among children with different preferences.
● Make it fun – some of the categories can be silly and others, thought provoking.
● Pass the speaking object around the circle and encourage the children to finish the sentence, *The thing that I like doing best is… .*

Middle phase
● Explain that the children didn't all change places at the same time because we are all different. Remind them that this is what makes each one of us special. We all like different things, but sometimes others will make us interested in something new. Then our list of favourite things can get longer and longer.
● Invite the children to turn to the child next to them and talk about something they enjoy doing. Ask them to explain how to do this activity and give reasons as to why it is such a favourite. In-school or out-of-school activities can be chosen.
● When the children have had sufficient time to talk about their favourite activity, ask for volunteers to stand up and tell the whole group about their chosen activity. Add some flourish by introducing each one as a 'sales pitch'!

Closing phase
● Congratulate the children for listening and speaking so well.
● Ask them to make sure that their feet are on the floor, their eyes are closed and their hands are in their laps. Take them on a short imaginary journey to somewhere warm and safe (such as the sofa at home, or tucked up in bed) and listen to a favourite story or piece of music. Encourage them to imagine themselves enjoying a cosy few moments.

Differentiation
Encourage younger children to think about some of their favourite things before the circle game activity by completing photocopiable page 23. Invite older children to demonstrate their listening skills by repeating as much as they can of their partner's description of an activity. For example, *My partner, Paul, says he likes computer games because… .*

I listen

AGE RANGE 5–7

LEARNING OBJECTIVE
To share their opinions on things that matter to them
and explain their views.

CURRICULUM LINKS
QCA citizenship: Unit 1 – Taking part; Unit 2
– Choices.
KS1: En1 Speaking and listening (3) Group discussion
and interaction.

What you need
Stick-on badges with smiley faces with big ears drawn on them.

What to do

Introductory phase
● Explain that the children are required to listen carefully for this circle game. Have all the children sitting on chairs.
● Now remove your own chair from the circle and give each child a number. Stand in the centre and call: *The postman is calling at 7 and 23.*
● The children with these numbers change places. If the call is *Collection time!* all the children change places. Try to reach a chair yourself during the change-over. The child left without a chair then becomes the caller.

Middle phase
● Tell the children that you will be doing research today on what makes a good listener.
● Go round the circle giving every child a partner. One child is 'red' and the other is 'blue'.
● Choose a colour (red) and ask all the 'red' children to talk about their favourite dinner. Tell the blue children that their job is to look away while the red children are talking.
● Ask for volunteer 'red' children to talk about whether it was hard or easy to keep talking to someone who wasn't looking at them.
● Choose another familiar subject such as favourite stories, my family, football and so on. Let the 'blue' and 'red' children take turns to listen to each other. Select different types of listening behaviour for them to exhibit. Examples of good listening include: eye-contact, nodding, smiling and leaning forward. Signs of poor listening include: interrupting, fiddling and wriggling, looking bored, humming and turning away.
● Ask for volunteers to describe how it feels when we are truly listened to and when we are ignored.
● Talk to the children about the new badges and tell them that you will be giving these out when you notice them using good listening skills. Remind them of what you will be looking for.

Closing phase
● Congratulate the children for listening so well to each other.
● Give their ears a few minutes' rest by asking them to sit comfortably, close their eyes, and concentrate on how their breath goes slowly in and out of their bodies.

Differentiation
Give younger children adult support when working in pairs. Older children can be given more complex subjects to talk about.

Circle Time **BRIGHT IDEAS**

AGE RANGE 7–9

LEARNING OBJECTIVES
To talk about opinions and explain views on issues
that affect themselves and society.

CURRICULUM LINKS
QCA citizenship: Unit 1 – Taking part; Unit 2
– Choices.
KS2: En1 Speaking and listening (3) Group discussion
and interaction.

Hot-seating

What you need
A 'speaking object' (see the
introduction on page 6).

What to do
Introductory phase
● Call out a four-word sequence
such as: *red, blue, yellow, green*. The
children in turn say *red, blue, yellow*
or *green* around the circle. The game
should be played as fast as possible.
● Pass the speaking object around
the circle and encourage the children
to finish the sentence, *My favourite
colour is… because… .*

Middle phase
● Thank the children for telling
everyone their favourite colour.
● Explain that the lesson is about
the children being able to talk about
their views and opinions.
● Put the children into small groups
and ask them to choose an animal
(or person/game) that they all know
something about.
● Ask each group to choose someone to sit in the 'hot-seat' with the other children
standing behind.
● Each group takes a turn to answer questions on the chosen topic (posed by the rest
of the class). If the child on the hot-seat wants a group member to answer, he raises his
hand and they swap seats.
● Ask the class to give their opinions about the views being expressed, but make sure
that they are aware that no put-downs or personal remarks may be made.
● You can also use hot-seating to discuss important issues. For example, ask the
children to pretend to be town planners (to discuss why you need a new park);
Ministers of Education (to discuss school-based issues); or big game hunters (to discuss
preservation issues)!

Closing phase
● Thank the children for sharing their knowledge, views and opinions.
● Bring the children together again by passing a smile and a handshake around the
circle. Smile at the child on your right and shake their hand. This continues until the
smile returns to you.

Differentiation
Help younger children by beginning the hot-seating session by sitting in the hot-seat
yourself to model how it works. Ensure that the children work in appropriate groups
so that all the children have the opportunity to express their views and opinions. More
able children can be hot-seated in a role to link with QCA Scheme of Work units in
geography or history such as taking the part of a Roman soldier or someone who lives
in a hot or cold place.

AGE RANGE 7–11

LEARNING OBJECTIVE
To contribute to class discussions that lead to
consensus, while maintaining and justifying a personal
viewpoint.

CURRICULUM LINKS
QCA citizenship: Unit 1 – Taking part; Unit 2
– Choices.
KS1 and KS2: En1 Speaking and listening (3) Group
discussion and interaction (4) Drama.

Leadership

What you need
A 'speaking object' (see the
introduction on page 6); flip chart.

What to do

Introductory phase
● Say a word, such as *King*. The
next child in the circle says a word
associated with it, such as *Crown*.
This continues around the circle.
● Pass the speaking object around
the circle and encourage the
children to finish the sentence, *If I
were the king/queen I would…* .

Middle phase
● Use the flip chart to make a list
of all the people who tell/show
them what to do – king, teacher,
football coach, parent, Prime
Minister and so on.
● Explain that all of these people
are leaders. Can they think of
any more leaders from history,
television or stories? Add them to
the list.

● Encourage the children to discuss the things that a good leader needs to be able to
do. Prompt if necessary.
● Ask them to remember situations when they didn't like being told what to do. Why?
Was it the way it was said or because it was unfair? Ask them to think about a time
when they felt happy to be told what to do.
● Make a list of the kind of leader we all like and another that describes bad leadership.
● Give the children a scenario where a leader is needed (such as a shipwreck, being
lost in the jungle, or something related to your current curriculum). Ask them (in small
groups) to make up a little play where one child leads them out of danger.
● Ask for volunteers who are willing to perform and discuss their plays.

Closing phase
● Congratulate the children for sharing their views about good leadership.
● Play the game, 'Leader of the Orchestra'. Start the game by pretending to play an
instrument. The children must copy and continue to 'play' the pretend instrument.
● Now walk round the outside of the circle. Without anyone seeing, gently touch one
child who will be the leader. The leader then takes over and changes the instrument
whenever they like.
● Everyone must also change instruments as soon as they notice. They must try to
guess who the new leader is!

Differentiation
Younger children can use the imaginary setting of familiar stories as a stimulus to think
about good and bad kings and queens. Let older children discuss times when they need
to be good leaders and followers, such as when looking after smaller siblings, when
playing football and when dealing with bullies.

AGE RANGE 9–11

LEARNING OBJECTIVE
To talk and write about opinions and explain views on issues that affect themselves and society.

CURRICULUM LINKS
QCA citizenship: Unit 1 – Taking part; Unit 2 – Choices.
NLS: Y4, T3, Text 16; Y6, T1, Text 13, T2, Text 15, T3, Text 13, 14;
KS1 and KS2: En1 Speaking and listening (3) Group discussion and interaction.

News round

What you need
A 'speaking object' (see the introduction on page 6); articles cut from newspapers; a blindfold.

What to do

Introductory phase
● Ask one child to leave the room. The rest of the class must then choose an adverb/ feeling such as: *proudly, slowly, sadly*.
● The child returns and tells the class to portray a particular action, such as brushing their hair in the manner of the chosen adverb. The player has to try to guess the word!
● Pass the speaking object around the circle and encourage the children to finish the sentence that includes one of the chosen adverbs used as a verb. For example, *I feel sad when…* , or *I feel proud when…* .

Middle phase
● Organise the children into groups of three or four (friendship groups are good for this). Ask the children to think about news items, either local or national, that make them feel uncomfortable or unhappy. They may use carefully selected articles cut from newspapers to remind them of issues.
● The groups report to the circle. The rest of the children in the circle can ask questions of the reporting group.
● In the same groups, ask the children to use the newspapers to find items that give them 'a feel good factor'.
● The groups report to the circle. The rest of the children in the circle can ask questions of the reporting group.
● Stress that reporters also have their own opinions, which can be reflected in how they present a story.

Closing phase
● Congratulate the children for sharing their views so confidently and for listening to each other.
● Explain that the final game is about listening.
● Ask for a volunteer to be blindfolded and to stand in the middle of the circle. Point to one of the children in the circle and ask them to whisper a simple sentence. The blindfolded child tries to guess where the voice is coming from and who it belongs to. Other children can be given turns.

Differentiation
The needs of your children will be addressed by the choice of newspaper stories. More able children can be encouraged to look at how the same story is reported in different newspapers.

AGE RANGE 7–11

LEARNING OBJECTIVE
To recognise their worth as individuals by identifying positive things about themselves and setting personal goals.

CURRICULUM LINKS
QCA citizenship: Unit 2 – Choices.
KS1 and KS2: En1 Speaking and listening (3) Group discussion and interaction.

Personal goals

What you need
A 'speaking object' (see the introduction on page 6); photocopiable pages 24 and 25; flip chart.

What to do

Introductory phase
● Alternately label the children 'orange' or 'lemon'. Call out either, *oranges* or *lemons*. The children change seats with the same fruit. If *fruit basket* is called, everyone changes places. Try to ensure that the children finish the game not sitting next to their friends.
● Ask each child to talk to the child on his or her right and tell each other about someone they admire.
● Explain to the children that they are going to introduce each other. Pass the 'speaking object' around the circle and encourage the children to finish this sentence: *This is... and she/he admires... .*

Middle phase
● Put the children in small groups and give each group one of the pictures of skilled people provided on photocopiable page 24.
● Ask each group to list the things that each person had to do to become skilled, such as practise, concentrate and so on.
● Ask each group to share their thoughts with the class. List their suggestions on the flip chart.
● Ask the children how they think success must feel for these people.
● Explain to the children that all the successful people had goals that they worked towards in order to succeed.
● Ask each child to think of a personal goal and think about the steps they can take to achieve it.
● Ask for volunteers to share their aspirations with the rest of the class.

Closing phase
● Explain that it is a good idea to regard reaching our goals as a series of small steps. Tell the children that they are all moving forward, all the time – so they have a great deal to feel proud about already.
● Tell the children that many successful people learn to 'see' themselves getting to their goal.
● Ask the children to sit quietly as you talk them through a little story where you 'see' some of them winning a prize or achieving an ambition. For example, *Let's all imagine that Paul wins a prize for his model-making. He would probably get his picture in the local newspaper...* and so on.

Differentiation
Ask younger children to think about who they would like to be if they were famous. Older children need to be encouraged to take a more realistic stance and consider what tasks they will need to do in order to attain their goals (see photocopiable page 25).

Circle Time

AGE RANGE 5–7

LEARNING OBJECTIVE
To recognise and name their feelings.

CURRICULUM LINKS
NLS: Y1 & Y2 vocabulary extension
KS1: En1 Speaking and listening (3) Group discussion
and interaction.

My feelings

What you need
A 'speaking object' (see the introduction on page 6); photocopiable page 26.

What to do

Introductory phase
● Alternately label the children 'wizard' or 'giant'. When either word is called, the children must change places.
● Add more interest to the movement by making reasons for each character to feel either angry, sad, or happy. For example, say: *The wizard has lost his magic book, so change places looking sad*, or, *Someone has eaten the giant's cake so he is feeling angry*.
● Pass the 'speaking object' around the circle and encourage the children to finish the sentence, *I feel happy when… .*

Middle phase
● Ask the children to name as many different feelings that they can think of. When a child names a feeling, ask all the children to demonstrate the feeling using their faces and bodies.
● Using photocopiable page 26, ask the children to think about how the children in the pictures are feeling and what might have happened to make them feel that way.
● Ensure that all the children have a chance to express their views.
● Ask the children to decide on a feeling they want to talk about and what makes them feel like that.
● Pass the 'speaking object' around the circle and encourage the children to finish the sentence, *I feel… when… .*

Closing phase
● Congratulate the children for talking about their feelings.
● Ask the children to think about how they are feeling during the week and what makes them feel happy, sad or angry.
● Tell the children that everyone is going to finish the session with a smile on his/her face!
● Ask the children to stand up. Choose one child to establish eye-contact and smile at another child. The child should then sit down and the smiled-at child then smiles at another child before sitting down.
● Continue until all the children are sitting down.

Differentiation
Naming and recognising feelings is difficult for some children. Ensure that you and these children practise using the vocabulary needed. Ask for volunteers to demonstrate acting out a feeling for the others to guess. Stories are a very good way to introduce young children to feelings and how to deal with them.

Dealing with feelings

AGE RANGE 5–7

LEARNING OBJECTIVE:
To recognise, name and deal with feelings in a positive way.

CURRICULUM LINKS:
NLS: Y1 & Y2 Vocabulary extension.
KS1: En1 Speaking and listening (3) Group discussion and interaction (4) Drama.

What you need

A 'speaking object' (see the introduction on page 6); music from *Cinderella* by Sergei Prokofiev; a version of the traditional story, 'Cinderella'; puppets and props to support the story (optional).

What to do

Introductory phase

● Tell the children the story of 'Cinderella'.

● Choose a feeling and show it on your face.

● Look at the child next to you and ask the child to mirror the face.

● After she has copied the face, that child moves her hand down over her face to remove the feeling. She then chooses her own facial expression which is then passed on to the next child, and so on around the circle.

● Show an excited expression on your face and ask all the children to identify the feeling.

● Pass the 'speaking object' around the circle and encourage the children to finish the sentence, *I feel excited when… .*

Middle phase

● Recap some important scenes from the story of Cinderella, focusing on how the characters must have been feeling to behave in the ways that they did.

● Put the children into small groups and give them each a different scene such as Cinderella feeling sad because she can't go to the ball.

● Ask the children to re-enact their scenes to show how each character was feeling (give puppets or toys to shy children and use costumes or props).

● In the correct order, ask each group to act out their scenes.

● Ask for advice on behalf of the characters. For example, what could the Ugly Sisters do to stop being so bad-tempered?

Closing phase

● Thank the children for sharing their wisdom.

● Explain that music can affect the way people feel. Play some to illustrate the point. Ask the children how the different pieces of music make them feel.

● Now say that you are going to play some music that might have been played at the ball. Ask the children to imagine themselves in the story as they listen.

Differentiation

Stories are a very good way to introduce young children to feelings. Encourage older children to use a range of words to describe the feelings of a chosen character in the story.

Circle Time

AGE RANGE 7–9

LEARNING OBJECTIVE
To recognise how to deal with their feelings towards themselves and others in a positive way.

CURRICULUM LINKS
KS2: En1 Speaking and listening (3) Group discussion and interaction (4) Drama.

Bad moods

What you need
A 'speaking object' (see the introduction on page 6); rainstick.

What to do
Introductory phase
● Tell the children that they can only use the numbers between two and nine. Start the process by saying a number, followed by the word *before* or *after*. For example: *four, after*. The child next to you must then say a number that comes after four.
● This child turns to the next child, repeats their number and says either, *before* or *after*. The second child decides on a number that fits the bill.
The object of the game is to continue until everyone has had a go. Using the 'speaking object', ask the children to complete the sentence: *Before I go to bed, I like to… .*

Middle phase
● Tell the children that you are all going to think about bad moods. Ask them to help you make a list of different kinds of bad mood. For example, stomping off when you lose a game. (Cite behaviours that you have observed in your own classroom.)
● Ask the children to describe how they think bad moods might feel, using examples of characters from stories or television programmes.
● Put the children into small groups and tell them that you want them to make up plays from given scenarios such as someone pushing in a queue; someone picking on someone else, and so on. Tell them that you want the play to focus on what happened before a bad mood was triggered!
● Ask the children to act out their plays.
● After each play, discuss the action that led to bad feelings. Ask the children to suggest ways in which the situation could have been avoided.

Closing phase
● Comment on the mature strategies for managing emotions that are suggested.
● Ask the children to listen to the rainstick. Give them a picture to visualise: the sea coming in over sand; the sun shining in a clear sky; the feel of sand and water on their toes; sitting in a garden on a summer's day.
● Bring the children 'back' and ask how they are feeling.

Differentiation
Let younger children act out scenes from stories using cloaks and crowns and witches' hats. Older children should enact very short plays and spend more time discussing strategies. This session is planned to avoid the possibility of anyone having to reveal anything personally distressing as this could be counter-productive.

AGE RANGE 7–11

LEARNING OBJECTIVE
To recognise how to deal with feelings in a positive way.

CURRICULUM LINKS
NLS: Y3–Y6 Vocabulary extension.
KS2: En1 Speaking and listening (3) Group discussion and interaction.

Positive and negative

What you need
A 'speaking object' (see the introduction on page 6).

What to do

Introductory phase
● Pass the speaking object around the circle and encourage the children to say (in a happy voice): *Hello my name is… and I am happy.*
● Introduce other feelings such as sad, excited, bored and angry. Ask the children to repeat the sentence in a voice demonstrating the new emotion.

Middle phase
● Explain that this lesson is about their feelings and how to cope with difficult emotions.
● Organise the class into four groups, each with a scribe.
Each group is given one word such as happiness, anger, fright, sadness, jealousy and boredom. Each group brainstorms their word to get as many other words as they can that relate to their key word. For example, sadness – alone, lonely, worried.
● The groups report back to the circle.
● Ask the children which emotions they think are the most difficult to deal with.
Explain that it is all right to have positive and negative feelings and that we are wise and mature enough to help one another find ways to manage difficult feelings.
● Ask if any children have strategies for dealing with the difficult emotions highlighted by the class.
● If the children find it difficult to suggest strategies for dealing with negative emotions make suggestions such as: talking about things; writing down concerns; taking deep breaths; crying; having a hug; exercise; listening to or making music; punching a pillow; yelling; stamping feet and clapping hands.

Closing phase
● The final game will leave the children laughing! Ask one child to stand in the centre of the circle.
● The other children take it in turns to ask the person in the middle questions, such as, *What do you comb your hair with?*. The child in the centre can only answer with the response: *sausages*. If the person in the centre laughs someone else must take their place, and so on.
● Limit the number of tries to asking each child three questions.

Differentiation
Ask the children to brainstorm their ideas about a specific feeling that is relevant to their age and maturity. Invite older, more able children to list the strategies that help to defuse a negative emotion and think of phrases to display in the classroom such as: *Calm Kids Cope!* and *Chill Out!*.

AGE RANGE 9–11

LEARNING OBJECTIVE
To recognise, as they approach puberty, how people's emotions change at that time and how to deal with feelings towards themselves, family and others in a positive way.

CURRICULUM LINKS
QCA science: Unit 5b – Life-cycles.
KS2: En1 Speaking and listening (3) Group discussion and interaction.

Mood swings

What you need
A 'speaking object' (see the introduction on page 6); photocopiable page 27.

What to do

Introductory phase
● Ask the children to stand up. Without speaking, safely act out something that makes them feel irritated, then angry or even furious!
● Pass the 'speaking object' around the circle and encourage the children to finish the sentence, *The feeling I don't like having is… .*

Middle phase
● Explain that this lesson is about how emotions can change during puberty.
● Explain that this stage in life is called adolescence and it is a time of great change.
● Ask them to describe the behaviour of teenagers they know or have seen on television.
● Put the children into small groups (same gender groups may be appropriate).
● Explain that you want them to draw what they think adolescence must feel like. Tell them that they must not draw pictures, but can only make patterns with any kind of lines (straight lines, zigzags, curls and so on).
● Demonstrate what you mean by drawing some lines and explaining your choices as you do so. For example draw some wavy, sleepy lines and explain that this is because you have noticed that adolescents sleep a lot. Then draw some spiky lines and say that you have noticed that adolescents can be irritable sometimes.
● Now ask the children to have a go. Ask them to think about what they have noticed and what they may be starting to feel themselves. Say: *Let those feelings go down your arm and into your hand to move the pen.*
● Ask them to work quickly without thinking too much. Give a time limit of five minutes.
● Ask for volunteers to share their abstract art and talk about why they have made their patterns in that way.

Closing phase
● Explain that smiling can be infectious and is often used to diffuse situations.
● Smile at the child on your right or left who then smiles at the next child, and so on around the circle until all the children are smiling. Encourage the children to remember eye-contact when smiling.

Differentiation
It is important to stress that puberty happens at any time between the ages of nine and 16. Be sensitive to the differences in the children in your class. Use photocopiable page 27 to help the class to visualise and talk about mood changes. Explain that it is very immature to be giggly about some of the changes that they can expect to see in children of the opposite gender.

AGE RANGE 5–7

LEARNING OBJECTIVE
To think about themselves, learn from their experiences and recognise what they are good at.

CURRICULUM LINKS
KS1: En1 (1) Speaking (2) Listening (3) Group discussion and interaction.

I am good at

What you need
A 'speaking object' (see the introduction on page 6); the ingredients to make a cake or pictures of different cakes; a plastic bag; sheets of paper and pencils.

What to do

Introductory phase
● Pretend to pass various things around the circle such as a kitten, a precious vase, a snake and a heavy case. Finish by passing round a real plastic bag.
● Ask the children to think about what could be in the plastic bag.
● Pass the 'speaking object' around the circle and encourage the children to finish the sentence, *In the bag there is… .*

Middle phase
● Explain that we are all different and that is why there were lots of different ideas about what was in the bag. Remind the children that they are special and unique.
● What do the children think 'unique' means?
● Show the children the cake ingredients and tell them that you could make any kind of cake with these ingredients.
● Ask them to think of a list of different kinds of cake – birthday, Christmas, fairy cakes and so on. Comment on how all the cakes are made from similar ingredients, yet are all different and delicious. Explain that the children are the same – all lovely, but different!
● Give out the sheets of paper and ask them to draw or write four things that make them special – brown eyes, long hair, calm manner, good at maths and so on.
● Ask for volunteers to come forward with their sheets and help them to see that they have chosen to draw a range of attributes – what they look like, things they are good at, their personality and so on. Be inclusive – saying for example: *Josie has drawn a picture of her curly hair. Has anyone else drawn their hair? Yes, Mark, you have drawn yours too. That's good.*

Closing phase
● Tell the children to take a deep breath and then let it out slowly.
● Say that they must never forget just how special and unique each one of them is.
● Now ask them to concentrate on feeling their toes and to give them a little wiggle. Repeat this with their fingers. Then ask them to slowly roll their necks and get rid of any tightness. Tell them to roll their shoulders and sit quietly for a few moments.

Differentiation
Encourage older and more able children to write a word or sentence to accompany their drawings.

AGE RANGE 7–9

LEARNING OBJECTIVE
To face new challenges positively by collecting information, looking for help, making responsible choices, and taking action.

CURRICULUM LINKS
QCA citizenship: Unit 2 – Choices.
KS2: En1 Speaking and listening (3) Group discussion and interaction.

Challenges

What you need
A 'speaking object' (see the introduction on page 6); enough small pieces of paper for each child to have a piece.

What to do

Introductory phase
● Give out the small pieces of paper.
● Ask the children to work in pairs. In turn, they have to tell the other person where to put the piece of paper – but only using their eyes to give directions.
● Tell the class that they have two minutes to complete the challenge.
● Ask the children how they felt during the game. Pass the 'speaking object' around the circle and encourage the children to finish the sentence, *During the game I felt… .*

Middle phase
● Explain that the lesson is about challenges. Ask what the word 'challenge' means to the children.
● Ask them to think of challenges that some children might have to face, such as changing schools, moving house, learning a new skill or performing in front of others.
● Ask volunteers to imagine how someone might feel just before they have to do something brave.
● Ask the children to share advice about how to help someone in each of these situations. Provide a sentence starter such as, *Would it help if… .*

Closing phase
● Explain that asking for help is one way to face a challenge and that the final game provides children with a chance to ask for and provide help.
● In this game, each child has to think of a food they could take to a party that begins with the first letter of their name. For example, *My name is Sally and I will bring sausages.* If they can't think of one, they may ask the class for help.
● Congratulate the class for discussing challenges and for being able to ask for and receive help.

Differentiation
With younger or less able children, use role-play to act out a situation that may be a challenge to them, either currently or in the future. The teacher should tease out the various strategies used to deal with the challenge. Invite older or more able children to list the challenges that face them in the future. Discuss strategies for helping them to take the right action.

AGE RANGE 7–9

LEARNING OBJECTIVE
To face new challenges positively by collecting information, looking for help and making responsible choices.

CURRICULUM LINKS
QCA citizenship: Unit 2 – Choices.
KS2: En1 Speaking and listening (3) Group discussion and interaction.

Challenge chant

What you need
A 'speaking object' (see the introduction on page 6); photocopiable page 28.

What to do

Introductory phase
● Challenge the children to play the first game at a furious pace!

● Put a spare chair into the circle. The children need to know which is the chair on their right. The leader calls a child's name and he/she moves to the empty chair. The child who now has the empty chair on their right now calls to a different child across the circle who moves to the empty chair. Continue until all the children have had a turn.

● Congratulate the children for facing up to the challenge of the game.

● Pass the 'speaking object'

around the circle and encourage the children to finish the sentence, *When I face a challenge I feel… .*

Middle phase
● Explain that everyone faces challenges in their lives and there are ways of facing challenges positively.

● Ask the children, in their pairs, what they would do if they were moving to another part of the country.

● Note the strategies as they are reported to the circle.

● Explain that often when children face new challenges they have to use various strategies, such as: seeing what other people do and copying them; tossing a coin; thinking of what they know about a situation; seeking accurate information; thinking of risks and consequences; accepting school or home rules and asking for advice.

● Ask them to think of a challenge that fits each strategy.

Closing phase
● Explain that sometimes we all need to ask for advice or support before we make a decision, and that it is important to know when and who to ask.

● Ask the children to help you to devise a class 'How to face a challenge chant'. For example: *Stop – think – choices – outcomes – decide.*

Differentiation
Use photocopiable page 28 and challenge more able children to do some research to find lists of people or organisations that provide information/advice. Ask the children to design a poster with the class 'challenge chant' on it.

AGE RANGE 10–11

LEARNING OBJECTIVE
To face new challenges positively by collecting information, looking for help, making responsible choices and taking action.

CURRICULUM LINKS
QCA citizenship: Unit 2 – Choices; Unit 12 – Moving on.
KS2: En1 Speaking and listening (3) Group discussion and interaction.

A new school

What you need
A 'speaking object' (see the introduction on page 6); paper and pencils.

What to do

Introductory phase
● Choose a child to be 'a caller' who stands in the middle of the circle. The children stand up and the caller says either: *All move left* or *All move right*. The children move along to their new chair and sit down.
● When the caller says: *All change!* every child changes seats with another child. The caller tries to find himself or herself a seat so that there is a new caller in the middle of the circle.
● When the children are confident with this game, the caller can say move any number of chairs to the right or the left.
● When the game is over, take some time to explain that during the game there were several changes of position and that the session is about positively facing new challenges or changes. The children will soon be transferring to a new school, which is a challenge. Ask if anyone can remember starting at this school.
● Pass the 'speaking object' around the circle and encourage the children to finish the sentence, *My first memory of (school name) is… .*

Middle phase
● Ask the children to tell you what made them feel settled in their current school.
● Organise the children into pairs to discuss how they think their life will be different in their new school.
● Explain that to face challenges in a positive way, the children need facts about the changes and what they can expect to encounter.
● Ask each child to list information they would like to know about their new school. Collect the lists and go through the queries. Some of them may be answered by others in the circle. If they are not, decide how the information will be obtained.
● Ask the children to think about what they are looking forward to at their new school.

Closing phase
● Pass the 'speaking object' around the circle and encourage the children to finish the sentence, *At my new school I am looking forward to… .*
● Congratulate the children for sharing their positive views.

Differentiation
Be sensitive to any fears about changing schools. Collect as much information as possible about the schools the children are moving to. Try to dispel any myths about what happens to new children at secondary schools.

New school – new friends

AGE RANGE 10–11

LEARNING OBJECTIVE
To face new challenges positively by collecting information, looking for help, making responsible choices, and taking action.

CURRICULUM LINKS
QCA citizenship: Unit 2 – Choices; Unit 12 – Moving on.
KS2: En1 Speaking and listening (3) Group discussion and interaction.

What you need
A 'speaking object' (see the introduction on page 6).

What to do

Introductory phase
● Call out different categories, such as: children who support the local football team; children who like to play computer games; children who like swimming and children who like cycling. Ask the children who fulfil these categories to stand up and change places with each other.
● Invite the children to think of other categories to use in the game.
● Now explain that during the game there were several changes of position. Ask the children what other more important changes have happened to them, such as moving house or changing classes.
● Pass the 'speaking object' around the circle and encourage the children to finish the sentence, *One change that has happened to me is … .*

Middle phase
● Explain that the lesson is about the transition to a new school, which will be a change and a challenge. One of the challenges may be having to find new friends.
● Organise the children into pairs and ask them to think about what sort of children they would like to have as friends. Ask the pairs to report back to the circle.
● Give the children time to think about how they are going to make new friends. Ask them what they think they need to do. Suggest, for example, that they should smile, look friendly, approach someone and start a conversation even if it is about the weather!
● Pass the 'speaking object' around the circle and encourage the children to finish the sentence, *To make new friends I would… .*
● Ask for volunteers to role-play the strategies they would use. Highlight the useful ideas from the role-plays.

Closing phase
● Ask the children how they will keep in touch with friends who are transferring to a different school.
● Invite the children to think how they should celebrate the end of their primary education. Pass the 'speaking object' around the circle and encourage the children to finish the sentence, *I think we should celebrate by… .*

Differentiation
Be sensitive to some of the children's fears about changing schools. Use role-play to act out the first day at a new school. If possible, invite Year 7 pupils to talk to Year 6 about their experiences at a new school.

Circle Time **BRIGHT IDEAS**

Likes and dislikes

- Write your name in the shield.
- Draw and label your favourite things.

Name:

My favourite food is:

My favourite book is:

My favourite place is:

My favourite toy is:

My favourite activity is:

Personal goals 1

Circle Time **BRIGHT IDEAS**

Personal goals 2

Name:
Date:

Three things I am proud of now:

A personal goal:
I will need help from:
Date I will achieve it:

A personal goal:
I will need help from:
Date I will achieve it:

A personal goal:
I will need help from:
Date I will achieve it:

My feelings

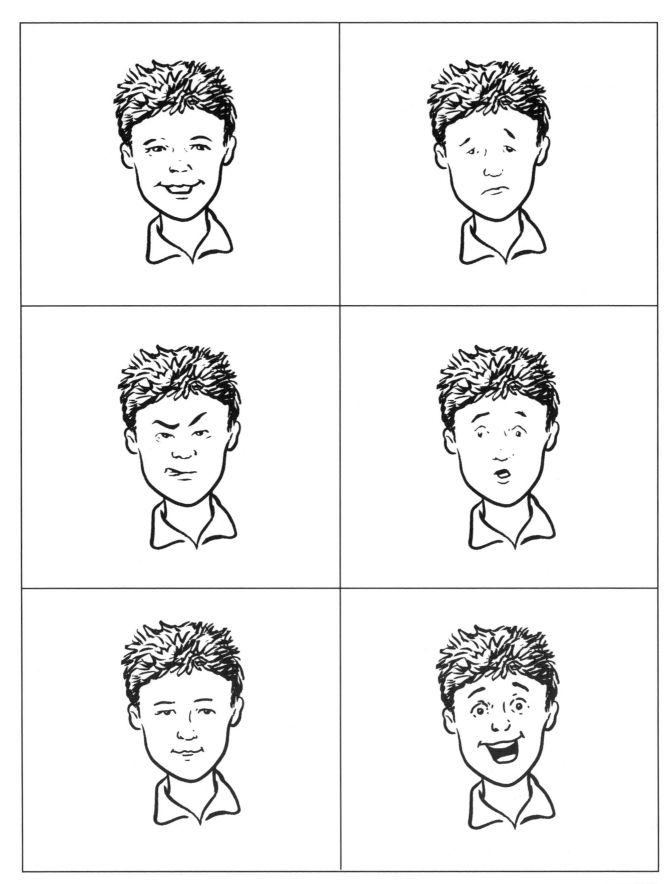

Mood swings

● In pairs, write down the feelings you have experienced or expect to experience as you go through puberty. You can use the examples given, as well as your own.

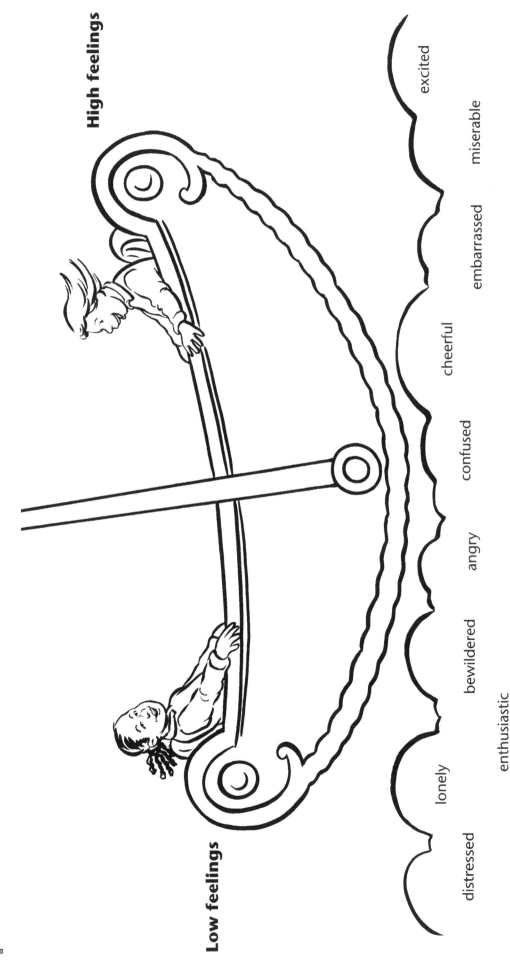

High feelings

Low feelings

excited

miserable

embarrassed

cheerful

confused

angry

bewildered

enthusiastic

lonely

distressed

Challenge chant

● Which strategies would you use to face these challenges?
● Write or draw what you would do on a piece of paper.

Circle Time **BRIGHT IDEAS**

CHAPTER 2

Preparing to be an active citizen

AGE RANGE 6–11

LEARNING OBJECTIVE
To research, discuss and debate topical issues, problems and events.

CURRICULUM LINKS
QCA citizenship: Unit 1 – Taking part; Unit 2 – Choices; Unit 6 – Developing our school grounds.
KS2: En1 Speaking and listening (3) Group discussion and interaction.

Where we live

What you need
A 'speaking object' (see the introduction on page 6); pens or pencils and paper.

What to do

Introductory phase
● Whisper a sentence to an adjacent child. The sentence is passed around the circle in a whisper. When the sentence returns to you (at the start), say the received and then the original version and compare them.
● Now ask the children to think of a piece of news – either something that relates to them or to their community.
● Pass the 'speaking object' around the circle and encourage the children to finish the sentence, *My news is… .*

Middle phase
● Explain that this lesson is about the community that the school is part of. Organise the class into small groups (friendship groups work well for this activity) and ask them to make lists of the things they like and the things they do not like about their community.
● Bring the groups back to the circle and allow each group to express their views to the circle.
● In groups, the children can then discuss how their community could be made safer and a better place for children to live in.
● Let the groups report back to the circle. Ask the children to then decide on one thing they would change about their community to make it a better place to live in, such as less cars, no smoking near children or more pavements.
● Pass the 'speaking object' around the circle and encourage the children to finish the sentence, *To make ………. a better place to live in I would… .*

Closing phase
● Congratulate the children for being able to communicate their views and for having such wonderful ideas.
● Whisper the name of a child on the other side of the circle. That child whispers someone else's name and so on. Then start another chain (while keeping the other one going) by calling a child's name.
● When two chains are established start a third – this time by singing a name across the circle. See how long the three chains can keep going!

Differentiation
The notion of community can be tailored to the age and abilities of the children so that younger children think about the close community, whereas older children can explore the wider community (such as the country they live in or the world). Let younger or less able children work as a pair rather than in a small group.

AGE RANGE 5–9

LEARNING OBJECTIVE
To understand why and how rules and laws are made
and enforced; why different rules are needed in
different situations and how to take part in making
and changing rules.

CURRICULUM LINKS
QCA citizenship: Unit 1 – Taking part; Unit 2
– Choices; Unit 8 – How do rules and laws affect me.
KS1 and KS2: En1 Speaking and listening (3) Group
discussion and interaction.

Rules

What you need
A 'speaking object' (see the introduction on page 6).

What to do

Introductory phase
● Call the name of a child in the circle and mime throwing a ball to them, they mime
catching the ball. The child with the imaginary ball says the name of another child who
mimes catching it. This continues until a name is called twice.
● Stop the game and ask if the game should be changed. Hopefully, someone will say
that to make it fair each child should have a turn (a rule should be added).
● Decide on the appropriate rule together. Continue to play.
● Congratulate the children for keeping to the rules of the game, and ask them to tell
you about other games that they play with rules.
● Pass the 'speaking object' around the circle and encourage the children to finish the
sentence, *I enjoy playing… .*

Middle phase
● Ask the children why rules are needed in school.
● Pass the speaking object around the circle and encourage the children to finish the
sentence, *We need rules in school because… .*
● Organise the children into pairs and ask them to decide on the most important
school rule, and what should happen if the rule is broken.
● Ask the pairs to report their ideas back to the circle.
● Ask the children if anyone would like to suggest a new rule for the school. Discuss
any ideas and, as a class, decide whether the suggestions should go forward to the
school council or other rule-making body.
● Remind the circle that it is necessary to have school rules so that everyone knows
how to behave and so that everyone feels happy and safe in school.

Closing phase
● Explain that the closing game
has rules, which must be kept if the
game is to be fair and enjoyable for
everyone.
● Say that each child only has one
'eek'. One child starts passing a
'zoom' around the circle by saying
Zoom and looking into the eyes of
the child on their right. This action
is repeated until a child uses their
'eek'. The player who says *Eek*
remains looking at the previous
player and the 'zoom' is passed the
opposite way around the circle.

Differentiation
Instead of school rules, discuss class
rules which may be more familiar
to the children. Encourage older
or more able children to design
appropriate ways of displaying rules.

Laws

AGE RANGE 9–11

LEARNING OBJECTIVE
To understand why and how rules and laws are made and enforced, why different rules are needed in different situations and how to take part in making and changing rules.

CURRICULUM LINKS
QCA citizenship: Unit 1 – Taking part; Unit 8 – How do rules and laws affect me?
KS2: En1 Speaking and listening (3) Group discussion and interaction.

What you need
A 'speaking object' (see the introduction on page 6); photocopiable page 46.

What to do

Introductory phase
● Send one child out of the classroom and ask the rest of the class to agree a rule about answering questions. For example: the children have to scratch their head before answering the question; each answer begins with a certain letter of the alphabet; each answer ends with another question.
● The child then returns to the circle and by asking simple questions (such as *What did you have for breakfast?*) tries to guess the rule.
● Ask the children to think about why rules are necessary.
● Pass the 'speaking object' around the circle and encourage the children to finish the sentence, *I think that rules are necessary because…* .

Middle phase
● Explain that the lesson is about rules and laws. Organise the groups of children into two or three to discuss a definition for rules and laws.
● Bring the groups together to discuss their definitions. Encourage them to reach the conclusions below.
● Give each child a copy of photocopiable page 46 to complete.
● Once they have completed the quiz, discuss any surprises that have emerged.
● Ask the children if they would change any of the laws.

Closing phase
● Reiterate to the children that they live in a democracy where laws are made by the elected Members of Parliament (MPs).
● The final game allows them to pretend to be a dictator. They can decide one law for their dictatorship.
● Pass the speaking object around the circle and encourage the children to finish the sentence, *If I ruled the world I would…* .

> ● A rule is part of a code of behaviour decided by groups of people and enforced by them.
>
> ● A law is recognised by the whole community as binding and is enforced by the government of the community.
>
> ● Laws are made by Parliament. If people break the law, they commit a crime.

Differentiation
Older or more able children could research other laws that interest them. Continue the theme by discussing laws the children would like to see implemented.

AGE RANGE 5–7

LEARNING OBJECTIVE
To recognise choices they can make, and recognise
the difference between right and wrong.

CURRICULUM LINKS
QCA citizenship: Unit 1 – Taking part; Unit 2
– Choices.
KS1: En1 Speaking and listening (3) Group discussion
and interaction.

Choices

What you need
A 'speaking object' (see the introduction on page 6); two books – one brightly coloured
and attractive looking but dull inside (such as an academic book), the other in a plain
cover but a good read or very attractive inside (you could cover one title in brown
paper); photocopiable page 47.

What to do

Introductory phase
● Ask the children to close their eyes and think of one person they would like to meet
– the person can be real or a character from a story. Ask them to think about why they
chose that person.
● Pass the 'speaking object' around the circle and encourage the children to finish the
sentence, *I would choose to meet… because… .*
● Congratulate the children for making a choice.

Middle phase
● Show the class the two books and ask which one they would like to read. Take a vote
to see which book is the popular choice.
● Open the books and explain that before making decisions they need to stop, think
and try to gather all the information they need to make a choice.
● Explain that sometimes choices involve making decisions about what feels right or
wrong, such as choosing where to play or how to behave in a certain situation.
● In small groups, ask the children to discuss a choice they, or a character from a book,
has had to make involving a right or wrong decision, for example, Goldilocks deciding
to eat the three bears' porridge.
● Ask the groups to report back to the circle.
● Congratulate the children for
sharing their ideas and for listening
to each other.

Closing phase
● Ask the children to help make up
a chant that involves right choices.
● Start the chant slowly and
gradually build up speed and
momentum, like a train pulling
away from a station until the final
'right' sounds like the train whistle.
For example:
Listening, listening, listening, listening
Being gentle (x4)
Kind and helpful (x4)
Working hard (x4)
RI-I-I-I-I-GHT!

Differentiation
Younger or less able children may
find it easier to discuss the scenarios
shown on photocopiable page 47.
Older children could write out some
of the scenarios they discussed and
then act them out to the class.

Circle Time

Right and wrong

AGE RANGE 5-7

LEARNING OBJECTIVE:
To recognise choices they can make, and recognise the difference between right and wrong

CURRICULUM LINKS
QCA citizenship: Unit 1 – Taking part; Unit 2 – Choices.
KS1 En1 Speaking and listening (3) Group discussion and interaction.

What you need
A 'speaking object' (see the introduction on page 6); photocopiable page 47 'Choices'.

What to do

Introductory phase
● Call out different choices, such as: *Would you rather read a book or watch TV?; Would you rather eat fruit or vegetables?* The children change seats with the children who make the same choices.
● Pass the speaking object around the circle and encourage the children to finish the sentence, *I would rather ... because... .*

Middle phase
● Explain that the choice the children made had no right or wrong answer, but sometimes there is a right or wrong choice to make. For example, choosing to cross the road at a pedestrian crossing or in the middle of a line of parked cars.

● Call out several right and wrong choices and ask the children to indicate by putting their thumbs up or down if they think they are right or wrong. For example, finding a bottle of cola in the park and deciding to drink it; getting into trouble and then telling a lie so you won't be blamed; seeing a toy left by another child and taking it to lost property.
● Ask the children for their own ideas for right and wrong choices.
● Show the children the photocopiable page 47 'Choices' and ask them to talk to a friend about the right and wrong pictures.

Closing phase
● Congratulate the children for thinking before reaching a decision. Emphasise that it is very important to think before taking action.
● Explain that the final game will enable the children to choose the right word or words to add to a class story.
● Start the story. Each child in the circle adds to the story. A word is the least they can add and a sentence the most. Provide the ending for the story yourself.

Differentiation
Help younger children to read the words under the empty boxes on photocopiable page 47, 'Choices'. Ask them to draw some pictures of a right and wrong choice. Invite older or more able children to discuss characters in books or on the TV who have made choices that turned out to be wrong, such as Goldilocks deciding to eat porridge that didn't belong to her. Ask them to write or draw their own story that involves right and wrong actions.

Circle Time

AGE RANGE 7–9

LEARNING OBJECTIVE
To realise the consequences of antisocial and
aggressive behaviours (such as bullying) on individuals
and communities.

CURRICULUM LINKS
QCA citizenship: Unit 1 – Taking part; Unit 7
– Children's rights/human rights.
KS2: En1 Speaking and listening (3) Group discussion
and interaction.

Bullying

What you need
A 'speaking object' (see the introduction on page 6).

What to do

Introductory phase
● Give one child a ruler and ask him or her to mime an action using the ruler as
another object, for example, an umbrella or a comb. The rest of the children need to
try to guess what the object is being used for. If the guess is right, the child doing the
mime says, *Well done*; if the guess is wrong they say, *Good try*. Once a child has guessed
correctly they take a turn to perform a different mime.
● After a number of mimes, point out that only positive responses are used in the
game (*Well done* and *Good try*).
● Ask how the children feel when negative or nasty things are said to them.
● Pass the 'speaking object' around the circle and encourage the children to finish the
sentence, *If a negative thing is said to me I feel… .*

Middle phase
● Explain that the lesson is about bullying.
● Ask what 'bullying' means. One definition is: *Repeated, deliberate, hurtful behaviour
and it is usually difficult for the victims to defend themselves.*
● Ask the children what they think a bully is.
● Pass the 'speaking object' around the circle and encourage the children to finish the
sentence, *A bully is… .*
● Organise the children into threes or fours to discuss what they think should happen
to prevent bullying in school.
● Ask the groups to report to the circle. It is important that the children realise that if
they are being bullied they should tell an adult.

Closing phase
● Explain that all children have
the right to feel safe and also
have the responsibility not to hurt
others.
● Ask for a volunteer to stand
in the middle of the circle. Ask
the other children to slowly and
calmly walk towards the child in
the middle. He or she can tell them
when to stop, for example when
the 'circle' has entered his or her
comfort zone. Repeat with other
volunteers.

Differentiation
To further the children's
understanding, use different
literature about bullying –
depending on the age and ability
of the children. Encourage the
children to make posters about
preventing bullying to be displayed
around the school.

Circle Time

AGE RANGE 7–11

LEARNING OBJECTIVE
To realise the consequences of antisocial and
aggressive behaviours (such as bullying) on individuals
and communities.

CURRICULUM LINKS
QCA citizenship: Unit 1 – Taking part; Unit 7
– Children's rights/human rights.
KS2: En1 Speaking and listening (3) Group discussion
and interaction (4) Drama.

Others' shoes

What you need
A 'speaking object' (see the
introduction on page 6).

What to do
Introductory phase
● Ask the children to think of
someone they would like to be for
the day.
● Pass the 'speaking object'
around the circle and encourage
the children to finish the sentence,
*If I could be someone else for a day I
would be… .*
● Ask the children to stand up and
walk around introducing themselves
to others in the circle as their
chosen character. They should try
to indicate the personality of their
character and talk about what the
character would talk about.
● Congratulate the children for
putting themselves into someone
else's shoes.

Middle phase
● Explain that this lesson is about antisocial behaviour. Part of the session is about
being able to think how it feels to be in the shoes of someone who is a victim of
antisocial behaviour.
● Put the children into pairs to discuss what they understand by the words 'antisocial
behaviour'.
● Ask the pairs to report back to the circle.
● Explain that bullying is one type of antisocial behaviour.
● Ask the children to discuss with their partner how they think it would feel to be in
the shoes of someone who is being bullied.
● Ask the pairs to report back to the circle again.
● Discuss what the victims should do. It is important to stress that children should
always tell a teacher if they are being bullied or know someone else that is.

Closing phase
● Stress that all children have the right to feel safe and that they have the responsibility
not to hurt others.
● Explain that after thinking about antisocial behaviour, the final game is going to be a
fun way to cheer the circle up. The idea is to create a 'Mexican wave'.
● Ask the children to place their hands on their knees. Start the wave by lifting your
arms in the air and then back onto your knees, the next person in the circle copies your
action, and so on in quick succession. With practice this can look very professional!

Differentiation
Careful pairing of children should be used to support less confident children during
the initial discussions. Suggest that older children write a piece about how to prevent
bullying from happening in their school.

AGE RANGE 9–11

LEARNING OBJECTIVE
To realise the consequences of antisocial and aggressive behaviours (such as bullying and racism) on individuals and communities.

CURRICULUM LINKS
QCA citizenship: Unit 1 – Taking part; Unit 7 – Children's rights/human rights.
KS2: En1 Speaking and listening (3) Group discussion and interaction (4) Drama.

Tell, tell, tell

What you need
A 'speaking object' (see the introduction on page 6).

What to do

Introductory phase
● Invite the children to walk around the room and tell as many individual people as possible what they had for their breakfast.
● Ask the children to repeat the process, but this time they should tell each person about an antisocial behaviour they know about.
● Pass the 'speaking object' around the circle and encourage the children to finish the sentence, *One type of antisocial behaviour I know about is… .*

Middle phase
● Explain that bullying is one type of antisocial behaviour.
● Ask the children what the three main types of bullying are. They are: physical, verbal and indirect (spreading nasty stories about someone or excluding them from groups).
● Ask why some children are victims of bullies. Emphasise the fact that bullies usually pick on children that can't or won't defend themselves. Bullies try to find something different about their victim to pick on, such as size, race, colour or academic ability.
● Discuss the concept that if race is an issue then that is called 'racism'. Ask the children what they think 'racism' means. One definition is: *Racism is bad feelings between people from different races.*
● Organise the children into groups of four or five and ask them to devise a role-play scenario involving one type of bullying.
● When watching the role-play, tease out the setting, the type of bullying and the strategies used to overcome it.

Closing phase
● Remind the children that they all have a right to be free from bullying and that a class or school can work towards being bully-free. Anyone who is being bullied should *tell, tell, tell.*
● Stress that groups of people working together can change situations for the better.
● Explain that the final game needs the class to work together to help other class members find a hidden object. Ask one child to go outside the room; and then hide a small object. The child outside comes back in and has to find the object. The class help by clapping louder when the seeker is close to the object. When they are far away from the object the clapping is very soft.

Differentiation
Encourage older or more able children to find out about the different organisations such as ChildLine that can provide help to children who are being bullied.

Circle Time

AGE RANGE 5–7

LEARNING OBJECTIVE
To realise that people and other living things have needs, and that they have responsibilities to meet them.

CURRICULUM LINKS
QCA citizenship: Unit 1 – Taking part; Unit 3 – Animals and us.
QCA science: Unit 1a – Ourselves; Unit 1b – Growing plants; Unit 2a – Health and growth.
KS1: En1 Speaking and listening (3) Group discussion and interaction.

What I need

What you need
A 'speaking object' (see the introduction on page 6); a plant (a potato plant would be ideal); photocopiable page 48.

What to do

Introductory phase
● Say or sing the rhyme: *One potato, two potato, three potato four, five potato, six potato, seven potato more* (traditional). The actions involve the children making a fist and putting their fists one on top of the other – every time a higher number of potatoes is said, the fists go higher and higher.
● Show the children your plant, and ask them what plants need to keep them healthy and growing.
● Pass the 'speaking object' around the circle and encourage the children to finish the sentence, *Plants need… .*

Middle phase
● Ask if any of the children have pets. Discuss what pets need to keep them happy and healthy.
● Reiterate that pets need food, water, a suitable place to live, companionship, and to be looked after by a vet if they are ill.
● Stress that if the children do have pets they have a responsibility to give their pets what they need to be happy and healthy.
● Ask the children to think about what they, themselves, need to be happy and healthy.
● Pass the 'speaking object' around the circle and encourage the children to finish the sentence, *One of the things that I need is… .*

Closing phase
● Remind the children of the need to look after their bodies to keep themselves healthy. Explain that the final game enables the children to think about various parts of their bodies.
● Ask the children to stand up in the circle. Explain that the children are going to pass different parts of their bodies around the circle!
● Start with toes; the first child gently touches the toe of the child next to him with his toe. She gently touches the toe of the child next to her with her toe. This action continues around the circle.
● When everyone has had a turn repeat with other parts of the body, such as knees, thumbs, elbows and fingertips.

Differentiation
Use photocopiable page 48 to help the children to draw on the needs of plants, pets and themselves. Younger or less able children will need help to distinguish between needs and wants. Ensure that all the children realise they need food, water, exercise, care, sleep and a suitable place to live if they are to thrive.

My responsibilities

AGE RANGE 5–7

LEARNING OBJECTIVE
To realise that people and other living things have needs, and that they have
responsibilities to meet them.

CURRICULUM LINKS
QCA citizenship: Unit 1 – Taking part; Unit 3 – Animals and us.
KS1: En1 Speaking and listening (3) Group discussion and interaction.

What you need
A 'speaking object' (see the introduction on page 6).

What to do

Introductory phase
● Label the children with three or four types of pet, such as dog, cat, fish and hamster. When their label is called, the children move across the circle in the manner of their pet name and change seats with the children with the same label.
● When the word *pets* is called, all the children change seats.
● Pass the 'speaking object' around the circle and encourage the children to finish the sentence, *If I could be a pet it would be a… because…* .

Middle phase
● Ask the children who have a pet to tell the rest of the circle what they do to look after it.
● Stress that pet owners have a responsibility to look after their animals' needs.
● Discuss the needs that children have.
● Organise the children into pairs and ask the pairings to talk about people who have special needs that need to be considered such as blind people or people in wheelchairs.
● Ask the pairs to report to the circle.
● Discuss the children's ideas and how the special needs of people can be met, for example improving access to buildings, labelling in braille and so on.
● Discuss the different organisations and charities that support people with special needs, such as KIDS and the National Deaf Children's Society.

Closing phase
● Tell the children that something as simple as a smile can brighten up another person's day.
● Smile at the child on your right or left who then smiles at the next child, and so on around the circle until all the children are smiling. Encourage the children to remember eye-contact when smiling.

Differentiation
Ensure that all children realise that people need food, water, exercise, care, sleep and a suitable place to live if they are to be happy and healthy. The age and ability of the children will determine the discussion; use appropriate books to develop the children's thinking. Be sensitive to children in the group who have special needs. Invite someone with special needs to talk to the circle about their needs and how others can help them. Encourage older or more able children to find out about different organisations and charities and their aims.

AGE RANGE 7–9

LEARNING OBJECTIVE
To reflect on spiritual, moral, social and cultural issues, using imagination to understand other people's experiences.

CURRICULUM LINKS
QCA citizenship: Unit 1 – Taking part; Unit 5 – Living in a diverse world.
KS2: En1 Speaking and listening (3) Group discussion and interaction.

We are all different

What you need
A 'speaking object' (see the introduction on page 6); photographs showing homes, schools and aspects of life from another country or place such as Chembakolli in India.

What to do

Introductory phase
● Call out different categories that several of the children have in common, such as, all the children who: like fruit; play a team game; do keep fit; feel tired; support Manchester United. The children who fulfil the category change places with each other in the circle.
● Pass the 'speaking object' around the circle and encourage the children to finish the sentence, *My favourite music is… .*

Middle phase
● Keep a mental check of how many different bands or types of music are mentioned and discuss with the children how they all think differently.
● Explain that the lesson is about understanding how different people feel and think in other parts of the world.
● Divide the children into groups of three or four. Using photographs of homes in a contrasting place, for example Chembakolli, ask the children to identify similarities and differences between the homes in the pictures and those in their own locality.
● Ask the groups to report to the circle.
● Using the same groups, the children should discuss photographs of the school in Chembakolli and their own school.
● Ask the children what it would be like to live in Chembakolli. Pass the 'speaking object' around the circle and encourage the children to finish the sentence, *If I lived in Chembakolli… .*

Closing phase
● Congratulate the children for being able to put themselves in someone else's shoes.
● Ask the children to imagine that they can give a gift to a child in Chembakolli.
● Pass the speaking object around the circle and encourage the children to finish the sentence, *My gift to a child in Chembakolli would be… because … .*

Differentiation
Help younger children by focusing on specific themes, such as comparing the types of material used to build the homes in each place. Make sure that older children think of at least two similarities between their homes and communities and those in your chosen contrasting locality.

AGE RANGE 7–9

LEARNING OBJECTIVE
To reflect on spiritual, moral, social and cultural issues, using imagination to understand other people's experiences.

CURRICULUM LINKS
QCA citizenship: Unit 1 – Taking part; Unit 5 – Living in a diverse world.
KS2: En1 Speaking and listening (3) Group discussion and interaction (4) Drama.

Our diverse world

What you need
A 'speaking object' (see the introduction on page 6); music from different cultures; a beanbag; a globe.

What to do

Introductory phase
● Give one child a beanbag and ask her to name a child that she has something in common with and then throw the beanbag to them. For example, *I like curry and so does Oscar.*
● Oscar then chooses something he has in common with someone else, for example, *I have a pet and so does Jessica*. Ensure that everyone in the circle is included.

Middle phase
● Explain that the lesson is about understanding how different people feel and think – particularly other people who live in different parts of the world.
● Ask the 'circle' if anyone has been on holiday where the way of life they saw was different from the way of life at home. Tease out the differences.
● Ask the children to think about stories about other countries they have seen in newspapers or on the television. Remind them that often, to be newsworthy, the story is a sad or bad one.
● Put the children into friendship groups and ask them to prepare a 'television report' from a chosen place in the world. One member of each group must play the role of a television reporter and ask the others questions about their country.
● Ask the groups to show their role-play to the circle.

Closing phase
● Congratulate the children for using their imaginations so well.
● Place the globe in the middle of the circle and ask the children to try and imagine the different experiences that children are having as they look at the different continents and countries.
● Play different pieces of ethnic music and ask the children to imagine themselves as part of the culture depicted in the music.

Differentiation
Encourage older or more able children to find out more information about the topical issues affecting other people in the world. They can then use this information in their TV role-play.

Circle Time **BRIGHT IDEAS**

AGE RANGE 5–7

LEARNING OBJECTIVE
To understand that we all belong to various groups and communities, such as family and school.

CURRICULUM LINKS
QCA citizenship: Unit 1 – Taking part.
KS1: En1 Speaking and listening (3) Group discussion and interaction.

I belong

What you need
A 'speaking object' (see the introduction on page 6).

What to do

Introductory phase
● Explain to the children that they are going to sing a song to the tune of 'Old Macdonald had a Farm'. Insert your own name on the first line (for example, Mrs Briggs):
Mrs Briggs has a band, E-I-E-I-O.
And in that band she has some claps, E-I-E-I-O.
With a clap, clap here and a clap, clap there,
Here a clap, there a clap, everywhere a clap, clap
Mrs Briggs has a band, E-I-E-I-O.
(Repeat, adding other body sounds such as a stamp, finger click or yawn).
● Explain that the lesson today is about belonging to groups and communities. Remind them that the class is a group that all the children belong to.
● Pass the 'speaking object' around the circle and encourage the children to finish the sentence, *The best thing about belonging to this class is… .*

Middle phase
● Explain that families are also groups. Stress that families are all different – some are much bigger than others; some families don't live together but others have relatives such as grandparents living with them. This subject will need to be treated sensitively.
● Ask the children to tell the rest of the circle about other groups they belong to (not school or family). Ask the children to say why they belong to them and to tell everyone a bit about the sort of activities that happen there.
● Now explain that the class is part of the larger group of the school community.
● Organise the children into pairs to discuss the people who belong to the school community.
● Ask the children to share their ideas with the circle.

Closing phase
● Comment on how much you enjoy belonging to the class group.
● Call out phrases that group the children in different ways, such as: *Whoever likes football come into the middle of the circle and jump up and down; Whoever likes chocolate come into the middle of the circle and smile at everyone!*
● The final statement should be: *Whoever is in my class come to the middle of the circle and shout, 'We are!'.*

Differentiation
Encourage older or more able children to make a list of the people that belong to the school community. Ask them to draw arrows between themselves and the different people that they are in direct contact with on a regular basis.

AGE RANGE 7–11

LEARNING OBJECTIVE
To resolve differences by looking at alternatives,
making decisions and explaining choices.

CURRICULUM LINKS
QCA citizenship: Unit 1 – Taking part.
KS2: En1 Speaking and listening (3) Group discussion
and interaction.

Conflicts

What you need
A 'speaking object' (see the introduction on page 6); musical instruments (optional).

What to do

Introductory phase
● Tell the children that by using either body parts or musical instruments, the circle
is going to create the sound of a conflict or argument. Begin to conduct the conflict,
which starts gently and gradually builds up and then calms down again.
● Pass the 'speaking object' around the circle and encourage the children to finish the
sentence, *My conflict or argument was about… .*

Middle phase
● Organise the children into groups of three or four. Ask the groups to discuss conflicts
or differences that characters in books or on TV have to deal with.
● Try to tease out the feelings of the characters when involved in the conflict and how
the conflict was resolved.
● Explain that not all differences of opinion become heated. In a democracy, voting is
often used as a way to make decisions.
● Relate this to your own school situation, for example, if you have a school council.
● Present the children with a situation to resolve as a group. If you have a suitable
scenario then use that, otherwise use the following: *Homework should be compulsory for
all school-aged children.*
● Ask for volunteers to speak for the motion and others to speak against it. The rest of
the circle should listen carefully.
● The children should elect a chairperson, or you can play that role.
● At the end of the discussion take a vote to reach a decision.

Closing phase
● Ask if the 'circle' would like to vote for a favourite final game or use the game
'Melting Candle' (described below) to end the session in a calm and peaceful manner.
● Ask the children to stand as rigid as a candle. Using a calm voice, tell the children
that the sun is gently melting them from the top to bottom. The children relax
gradually until they are a lump of wax on the floor.

Differentiation
Younger and less mature children may need more sessions on how to control their
anger if they are in a conflict situation; the notion of having a private STOP sign is a
good one to practise with them.

Circle Time **BRIGHT IDEAS**

AGE RANGE 9–11

LEARNING OBJECTIVE
To recognise the role of voluntary, community and
pressure groups.

CURRICULUM LINKS
QCA citizenship: Unit 1 – Taking part.
KS2: En1 Speaking and listening (3) Group discussion
and interaction.

Pressure groups

What you need
A 'speaking object' (see the
introduction on page 6);
photocopiable page 49.

What to do

Introductory phase
● Ask the children to stand up
in a space. Ask each child to see
how far he or she can lean over
backwards without falling.
● Now invite the children to
find a partner and repeat the
exercise – taking it in turns
to support each other. The
children should see a difference
when working in a pair.
● Explain that a pair is a small
group and pairs can often
achieve more together than
alone. Ask the children to think
of activities they enjoy doing in
a group.
● Pass the 'speaking object' around the circle and encourage the children to finish the
sentence, *An activity I enjoy doing with a group is… .*

Middle phase
● Explain that the lesson is about the role of voluntary, community and pressure
groups. Discuss with the children why people form or join these types of groups.
● Explain that some groups are formed to make a difference or contribute to their
community. Ask the class to think of some of the groups that they know about.
● Pass the 'speaking object' around the circle and encourage the children to finish the
sentence, *One group that makes a difference in the community is… .*
● Organise the children into threes or fours to invent their own group. Give out copies
of photocopiable page 49 so that the groups think about the same criteria.
● Ask the groups to report to the circle.

Closing phase
● Congratulate the children for behaving in a mature and responsible way and for
cooperating.
● Stress the need for groups to work together if they are to succeed. Tell them that the
final game is also like that!
● Ask five children to stand in the middle of the circle. At the command *Pins down*
some or all five children or 'pins' return to their seats. Other children must replace
them so that there are always five 'pins' in the circle. The game depends on the class
cooperating to maintain the five pins.

Differentiation
Ensure that each small group has a mixture of abilities so that one child can be the
scribe. More able children could find out about specific groups and decide how to
present the information to the class.

AGE RANGE 7–11

LEARNING OBJECTIVE
To explore how the media present information.

CURRICULUM LINKS
QCA citizenship: Unit 1 – Taking part; Unit 11 – In the media.
KS2: En1 Speaking and listening (3) Group discussion and interaction.
NLS: Y3–6 Text level work: Non fiction, reading comprehension.

News

What you need
A 'speaking object' (see the introduction on page 6); a wide selection of newspapers from the same day, carefully vetted to remove inappropriate stories; photocopiable page 50.

What to do

Introductory phase
● Ask each child to contribute between three to six words to a news item, developing the story as it progresses around the circle. The teacher may start with: *Today in … .* If the news item ends, the next participant begins a new one.
● Pass the 'speaking object' around the circle and encourage the children to finish the sentence, *I like news stories that are about… .*

Middle phase
● Organise the children into groups of three or four. Ask the groups to look through the carefully vetted newspapers to find photographs and headlines that interest them.
● Ask the groups to report back to the circle and to say what the main news of the day was in their newspaper.
● Choose one of the main stories and ask the groups to find it in their newspaper.
● Using the newspapers, look at the same story but note the different headlines, and also the presentation.
● Choose a fictional story that all the children know, for example, 'Cinderella', and ask the groups to design a headline for the story.
● Compare the results by passing the 'speaking object' around the circle and encourage the children to call out their headlines.

Closing phase
● Remind the children that television, radio and the internet also report news.
● Explain that the final game encourages the children to think about who might have said various things.
● Ask one child to leave the room. Ask three or four children to make positive statements about the child. When the child returns, he or she should stand in the middle of the circle, while the teacher repeats the statements. The child must then try to guess who said what about them.

Differentiation
Use photocopiable page 50 to encourage the children to write a news story based on their headline. Less able children can focus on the headline. Older or more able children can study the newspaper articles in more detail to note differences in the reports, as well as facts and opinions.

AGE RANGE 7-11

LEARNING OBJECTIVE
To explore how the media present information.

CURRICULUM LINKS
QCA citizenship: Unit 1 – Taking part; Unit 11 – In the media.
KS2: En1 Speaking and listening (3) Group discussion and interaction.
NLS: Y3–6 Text level work: Non fiction, reading comprehension.

Adverts

What you need
A 'speaking object' (see the introduction on page 6); a wide selection of newspapers and magazines; leaflets from local doctor's surgery.

What to do

Introductory phase
● Ask the children to imagine that they are up for sale! Invite them to think of three adjectives to describe themselves to use in an advert to sell themselves!
● Pass the 'speaking object' around the circle and encourage the children to finish the sentence, [*Name of child*] *is... .*

Middle phase
● Organise the children into friendship groups of two or three. Using the newspapers and magazines, give the groups between three and five minutes to find an advert that appeals to them. Suggest that they find something that would influence them.
● Ask the groups to report back to the circle, explaining why they made the choices they did.
● Take a vote to decide which advert the class feels is the most persuasive and then discuss why.
● Ask the children to think about their favourite advert and whether it caused them to buy or do whatever the message was persuading them to do.
● Explain that the media is also used to promote health messages. Ask the groups to find examples in the papers and magazines, or use the leaflets from the doctor's surgery. For example, 'Smoking damages your health'; 'Sunbathing can cause skin cancer'; 'Don't drink and drive'.

Closing phase
● Explain that the final game is also about passing on messages. The idea of the game is to pass a message around the circle.
● Zip is passed around the circle by saying *Zip* and holding both palms up and pointing towards the next person in the circle. Saying *Bong* and holding up two hands in a 'halt' gesture changes the direction of the message. The message goes elsewhere in the circle when *Zap* is said and both hands are pointed at the recipient with palms together. Each child can only say *Zap* and *Bong* once, but can say *Zip* any number of times!

Differentiation
Suggest that older children look for common phrases in the adverts, such as 'New and improved' or 'Buy now!'. Encourage older and more able children to begin to recognise when their decisions are being manipulated by adverts.

Laws

● Read the statements. Circle the word 'True' or 'False' for each one.

1. It is against the law to sell tobacco to children under the age of 16.

      True   False

2. There is a single date when young people can leave school and take a full-time job.

      True   False

3. By law you have to wear a cycle-helmet when riding a bicycle.

      True   False

4. The legal age for buying alcohol is 21.

      True   False

5. It is illegal to have a hand-held mobile phone in a car.

      True   False

6. Children from the age of ten are legally responsible for their actions.

      True   False

7. You can be sent to a Juvenile Justice Centre from the age of ten to 16 inclusive.

      True   False

8. Leaving or depositing litter is against the law.

      True   False

9. You can get married at 16.

      True   False

10. You can be called to serve on a jury from your 18th birthday.

      True   False

11. You can buy fireworks from shops from the age of 12.

      True   False

Answers
1. True. 2. True – the only leaving date is the 30 June. You must be 16 on or before 1 July in the year you want to leave. 3. False. 4. False – the legal age is 18. 5. False – it is illegal to *drive* and use a hand-held phone. 6. True. 7. True. 8. True – people can be fined up to £2500. 9. True – only with parents' consent, otherwise the age is 18. 10. True. 11. False – you need to be 16.

Choices

Playing in the street amongst traffic.

Playing in the park.

Putting litter in the bin.

Dropping litter.

A wrong choice

A right choice

What I need

● Draw what a plant and a pet need to be healthy.

Draw a picture of yourself and the things you need to be happy and healthy.

Circle Time **BRIGHT IDEAS**

Pressure groups

Constitution of

....

The aims of the group are:

How the group will fulfil its aims:

People eligible to join the group:

Subscription fees:

How often the group will meet:

Who will call the meetings:

The group's logo:

News

THE DAILY NEWS

Heading

Sub- head

Circle Time **BRIGHT IDEAS**

CHAPTER 3

Keeping healthy

AGE RANGE 5– 7

LEARNING OBJECTIVE
To make simple choices that improve health and well-being.

CURRICULUM LINKS
QCA science: Unit 1A – Ourselves; Unit 2A – Health and growth.
KS1: En1 Speaking and listening (3) Group discussion and interaction.

We are what we eat

What you need
A 'speaking object' (see the introduction on page 6); photocopiable page 68.

What to do

Introductory phase
● Label the children alternately 'apple' or 'pear'. Call out either *apples* or *pears* – and ask the children to change seats with the same fruit. If *fruit basket* is called, all the children change seats.
● Ask what other fruits the children like to eat. Pass the 'speaking object' around the circle and encourage the children to finish the sentence, *The fruit I like to eat is… .*

Middle phase
● Explain that fruit and vegetables are good things to eat. We should eat five pieces a day. They help us to stay healthy.
● Discuss what being healthy means.
● Explain that it is important to eat different foods to provide our bodies with a balanced diet to stay healthy. We should eat less of some foods. The foods we should eat less of are those with sugar, like sweets, and food with too much fat, like chips or crisps. These foods should be eaten rarely. Healthy food such as fruit, vegetables, pasta, brown bread, yoghurt, fish and meat can be eaten more often. Explain that water is also part of a healthy diet.
● Organise the children into pairs and ask them to discuss their favourite foods. Ask them to decide which of the foods that they like are healthy and can be eaten frequently.
● Pass the 'speaking object' around the circle and encourage the children to finish the sentence, *The healthy food I would choose to eat is … .*

Closing phase
● Congratulate the children for knowing which foods are healthy and explain that the final game is all about five pieces of fruit or vegetables per day.
● Ask the children to listen the first time and then copy the rhyme and rhythm. Start the chant slowly and gradually build up speed, like a train pulling away from a station, until the final 'mango' sounds like a train whistle:
Carrots and peas, carrots and peas, carrots and peas, carrots and peas,
Apples and pears, apples and pears, apples and pear, apples and pears,
Bananas, bananas, bananas, bananas,
M-a-n-g-o!

Differentiation
Give children a copy of photocopiable page 68 and ask them to draw or write what they should put in their bodies for a healthy dinner. Provide less able children with pictures of food and drink for them to choose healthy options to stick onto the body.

Staying healthy

AGE RANGE 5–7

LEARNING OBJECTIVE
To make simple choices that improve health and well-being.

CURRICULUM LINKS
QCA science: Unit 1a – Ourselves; Unit 2a – Health and growth.
KS1: En1 Speaking and listening (3) Group discussion and interaction.

What you need
A 'speaking object' (see the introduction on page 6).

What to do

Introductory phase
● Ask the children to walk around inside the circle. They should all walk slowly, looking down. They should not look at or bump into anyone else.
● Touch a child gently on the shoulder. Invite the child to look up and then smile at each other. The child then sits down. Continue until every child has had a turn (in a big class it is a good idea to have two people touching).
● Pass the 'speaking object' around the circle and encourage the children to finish the sentence, *When I am smiled at I feel…* .

Middle phase
● Explain that most people feel happy when they are smiled at. A happy person is easy to recognise but what is a healthy person?
● Pass the 'speaking object 'around the circle and encourage the children to finish the sentence, *A healthy person is…* .
● Discuss the children's answers.
● Organise the children into groups of two or three and ask them to discuss what they do to keep healthy.
● Ask the groups to report back to the circle.
● Discuss the healthy choices that the children can make, such as cleaning their teeth properly; having enough sleep; taking exercise; drinking plenty of water; eating a balanced diet.

Closing phase
● Congratulate the children for knowing so much about staying healthy.
● Explain that the final game is about exercise. Each child should think of one exercise they like to take part in. The children can then take it in turns to say and mime doing the exercise.

Differentiation
Develop a set of exercise mimes for younger children to identify and copy. Encourage older and more able children to talk in more detail about their exercise, explaining what it involves and why it is good for them.

Circle Time

Healthy choices

AGE RANGE 7–11

LEARNING OBJECTIVE
To know what makes a healthy lifestyle, including the benefits of exercise and healthy eating.

CURRICULUM LINKS
QCA science – Unit 3a: Teeth and eating; Unit 5a – Keeping healthy.
KS2: En1 Speaking and listening (3) Group discussion and interaction.

What you need
A 'speaking object' (see the introduction on page 6); photocopiable page 69.

What to do

Introductory phase
● Call out the names of different foods and ask all the children who like the food to change places in the circle.
● Pass the 'speaking object' around the circle and encourage the children to finish the sentence, *My favourite food is… .*

Middle phase
● Discuss why we all need food to survive and the notion of a balanced diet.
● Discuss what other things make up a healthy lifestyle.
● Explain that exercise is an important part of maintaining a healthy mind and body. In pairs, ask the children to think of as many ways as possible to exercise.
● Ask the children to think of the healthy choices they make (such as playing football after school, rather than watching television). Pass the 'speaking object' around the circle and encourage the children to finish the sentence, *One healthy choice I make is to… .*
● In their pairs, ask the children to discuss ways they could change their lifestyle to improve their health.
● Ask the pairs to report to the circle again.

Closing phase
● Explain that the children need to begin to take some responsibility for their health, rather than relying on parents or carers.
● Place an imaginary box in the middle of the circle and invite a child to come to the box and take out some food. The child mimes eating the food, while the rest of the circle try and guess the food. Did the child choose a healthy or unhealthy option?

Differentiation
Give out copies of photocopiable page 69. Suggest that younger or less able children draw their responses. The meals should contain; a third fruit and vegetables; a third bread, cereal or potatoes; and the remaining third from meat, fish or an alternative such as eggs or beans – with dairy products and a little fat and sugar. Water is an ideal drink. Encourage older or more able children to present the results of 'favourite foods' as charts or tables. To extend the work ask these children to find out how different types of food affect their bodies.

Circle Time

AGE RANGE 7–11

LEARNING OBJECTIVE
To know what makes a healthy lifestyle including physical and mental well-being.

CURRICULUM LINKS
QCA science: Unit 3a – Teeth and eating; Unit 5a – Keeping healthy.
KS2: En1 Speaking and listening (3) Group discussion and interaction.

Healthy people

What you need
A 'speaking object' (see the introduction on page 6).

What to do

Introductory phase
● Ask the children to draw an '8' in the air, in front of themselves. Suggest that they use one hand and then change to the other.

● Now ask the children to close their eyes and draw a lazy '8', (a figure '8' laying on its side). Introduce some humming or singing as they do this. The tune, 'Yellow Submarine' is a good one to use.

● Explain that drawing the lazy '8' whilst humming or singing can be very relaxing. Ask the children what else they do to help them to relax.

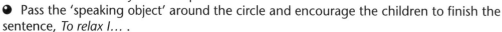

● Pass the 'speaking object' around the circle and encourage the children to finish the sentence, *To relax I… .*

Middle phase
● Explain that this lesson is about a healthy lifestyle.
● Ask the children to think of two famous people; one that they think has (or had) a healthy lifestyle and one who they think does not.
● Pass the 'speaking object' around the circle and encourage the children to finish the sentence, *I think… has a healthy lifestyle and that … does not.*
● Ask the children to think of the attributes that make a healthy person.
● Explain that being healthy is not just about the body, but also about mental health. It is about being happy and positive about life.
● Ask the children to think of themselves doing things that make them feel happy and positive.
● Pass the 'speaking object' around the circle and encourage the children to finish the sentence, *I feel happy when… .*
● Explain that feeling happy is important to good mental health. Remind them that being healthy is about mental and physical well-being.

Closing phase
● Congratulate the children for knowing so much about a healthy lifestyle.
● Explain that the final game will leave the children feeling very relaxed.
● Ask the children to stand as rigid as a candle. Using a calm voice, tell the children that the sun is gently melting them from top to bottom. The children should relax gradually until they are a lump of wax on the floor.

Differentiation
Some children may need to discuss things with a friend before completing a sentence or round. Try hearing from the confident children first, taking a break and then inviting the less confident children to make their contributions.

Circle Time **BRIGHT IDEAS**

Keeping clean

AGE RANGE 5–6

LEARNING OBJECTIVE
To maintain personal hygiene.

CURRICULUM LINKS
QCA science: Unit 1a – Ourselves.
KS1: En1 Speaking and listening (3) Group discussion and interaction.

What you need
A 'speaking object' (see the introduction on page 6); photocopiable page 70.

What to do

Introductory phase
● Start by singing the chorus of 'Here We Go Round the Mulberry Bush' (traditional), inviting the children to join in with you. After the chorus, sing verses about personal hygiene such as: *This is the way we … wash our hands/clean our teeth/have a bath/use a tissue/brush our hair.*
● Pass the 'speaking object' around the circle and encourage the children to finish the sentence, *I wash my hands before/after … .*

Middle phase
● Ask the children to demonstrate how they wash their hands.
● Ask for a volunteer to talk through the actions.
● Explain that it is very important to wash hands after using the toilet and before food is touched or eaten. Ask the children to think about all the things their hands do in a day that cause them to get dirty.
● Ask the children to feel their teeth with their tongues. Encourage them to feel the different types of teeth they have.
● Ask the children if they know why it is important to keep their teeth clean.
● Invite the children to demonstrate cleaning their teeth.
● Tell the children you are going to suggest some good and bad habits that relate to keeping clean. Ask them to smile and raise their thumbs for good things and to frown and signal 'thumbs down' for bad things. Suggest things such as: cleaning teeth; wiping noses on sleeves; coughing without covering their mouths; having a bath and so on.

Closing phase
● Explain that to stay healthy we try to keep germs out of our bodies. That's why we need to think about keeping clean.
● Explain that you are going to pass some pretend food around the circle, so the children need to pretend to wash and dry their hands.
● Pretend to pass food from one child to another around the circle. For example, jelly, toast, boiled egg and a plate of curry.
● Give out copies of photocopiable page 70 and ask the children to draw what they do at home in order to keep clean.

Differentiation
Ensure that younger children know what to do in a lavatory. Take them and a teddy into the lavatory and use teddy to demonstrate what to do. Put pictures in the lavatories to remind them how to behave.

Coughs and sneezes

AGE RANGE 5–7

LEARNING OBJECTIVE
To know how some diseases spread and how they can be controlled.

CURRICULUM LINKS
QCA science: Unit 1a – Ourselves; Unit 2a – Health and growth.
KS1: En1 Speaking and listening (3) Group discussion and interaction.

What you need
A 'speaking object' (see the introduction on page 6); materials to make a poster.

What to do

Introductory phase
● Explain that you are going to play a game called 'Catch a smile'.
● Ask all the children to stand up. Choose a volunteer to establish eye-contact and smile at another child. That child then sits down and the smiled-at child smiles at another child before sitting down, and so the game continues. The game is over when all the children are sitting down.
● Congratulate the children for 'catching the smile' and ask them what else they can catch.
● Pass the 'speaking object' around the circle and encourage the children to finish the sentence, *I can catch a … .*

Middle phase
● Ask the children if they have ever caught a cold.
● Discuss other illnesses the children have had (be sensitive to individual circumstances).
● Ask the children to think about which of the common illnesses are catching or can be spread from child to child.
● Explain that illnesses can be spread by: coughs and sneezes; flies and insects; food and water; unwashed hands; and animals.
● Organise the children into pairs. Invite each pair to make a poster showing one way that disease can be spread.
● Discuss what the children can do to help to control the spread of diseases.

Closing phase
● Explain that people often feel tired when they are ill, and the final game provides the chance for the children to think about how they feel when they are running out of energy.
● Tell the children to be wind-up toys! Explain that they have just been wound up, so they are full of energy! The children move around the circle until their mechanism starts to run down. They gradually move more and more slowly until they are asked to gently sit back in their chairs.

Differentiation
Younger or less able children will need support to make their posters. Show them some examples of health posters to give them inspiration. Challenge older children to identify areas of the classroom or school where good hygiene is important. Ask them to target their posters for display in these areas.

AGE RANGE 9–11

LEARNING OBJECTIVE
To be aware of which commonly available substances and drugs are legal and which are illegal and know about their effects and risks.

CURRICULUM LINKS
QCA science: Unit 5a – Keeping healthy.
KS2: En1 Speaking and listening (3) Group discussion and interaction.

Drugs

What you need
A 'speaking object' (see the introduction on page 6); A3 sheets of paper; pens or pencils.

What to do

Introductory phase
● Tell the children that you have placed an imaginary box in the middle of the circle. Ask the children to take turns to go up to the box and take out an imaginary object and demonstrate its use. The rest of the circle must guess what the object is.
● Ask the children to imagine that there was a drug in the box. What could it be?
● Pass the 'speaking object' around the circle and encourage the children to finish the sentence, *The drug in the box could be… .*

Middle phase
● Explain that this lesson is about 'drugs. Provide the children with a simple definition of what you mean by the word 'drugs'. One definition is: *Drugs are substances that affect how a person thinks, feels or behaves.*
● Ask the children to think about a legal drug that they have taken such as prescribed medicines, coffee and cola.
● Organise the class into groups of three or four children, giving each group a large sheet of paper. Ask them to write the word 'Drugs' in the centre of the sheets of paper. Working in their groups, they should then write all the words they know associated with drugs around the word.
● Ask the groups to report back to the circle. Talk about the risks involving drugs.
● Ask the children what information they are unsure about; do they know which drugs are legal and which are illegal?
● What other information would they like to know? (You should note any questions.)

Closing phase
● Thank the children for sharing their knowledge about drugs and reassure them that future lessons will deal with their general questions.
● Explain that the final game also involves asking questions. Tell the children that you are thinking about one of the children in the circle. Invite the children to ask you questions to try and guess the child you are thinking about. Explain that you will only answer *Yes* or *No*. Repeat the game several times.

Differentiation
This is a needs-analysis lesson. The children's responses will determine the needs of the class and will enable you to prepare relevant lessons for them. Ensure that the groups are of mixed ability so that each group contains confident writers and spellers, if possible.

AGE RANGE 9–11

LEARNING OBJECTIVE
To be aware that medicines are drugs and to know about their effects and risks.

CURRICULUM LINKS
QCA science: Unit 5a – Keeping healthy.
KS2: En1 Speaking and listening (3) Group discussion and interaction.

Medicines

What you need
A 'speaking object' (see the introduction on page 6); paper and pens; samples of empty medicine containers with patient leaflets.

What to do
Introductory phase
● Say a word, such as, *leaf*. Ask the next child in the circle to say a word associated with it, such as *tree*. Continue around the circle. Introduce a rhythm by adding two claps between the words, such as: *leaf* clap, clap; *tree* clap, clap …
● Now ask the children what their response would have been if you had started the game with the word, *drug*.
● Pass the 'speaking object' around the circle and encourage the children to finish the sentence, *To the word 'drug', I would say… .*

Middle phase
● Remind or tell the children of the simple definition of drugs: *Drugs are substances that affect how a person thinks, feels or behaves.*
● Explain that this lesson is about legal drugs, including medicines.
● Ask if anyone knows what legal drug is found in tea, coffee, cocoa, chocolate, and some soft drinks (caffeine).
● Discuss how caffeine affects the body. Introduce the word 'stimulant' and talk about how it makes people feel alert. Explain that caffeine is also used in some medicines because it stimulates the heart.
● Organise the class into groups of two or three children. Give each group a clean, empty medicine container and leaflet. Ask the children to examine the container and leaflet and to write down two or three interesting facts.
● Ask the groups to report back to the circle and then discuss the risks associated with taking medicines.

Closing phase
● Remind the children that they should only use medicines given to them by a responsible adult (such as a carer, family member or teacher).
● Explain that the final game is based on something that lots of people like to put into their bodies – sausages!
● Ask one child to stand in the centre of the circle. The other children take it in turns to ask questions, such as: *What do you comb your hair with?* The child in the centre can only answer with *Sausages!* If the person in the centre laughs they must change places with someone else. Limit the number of tries to three for each child.

Differentiation
Younger or less able children may need support to read the information on the medicine leaflets. Provide adult support or organise the groups accordingly.

Circle Time **BRIGHT IDEAS**

Cigarettes and alcohol

AGE RANGE 9–11

LEARNING OBJECTIVE
To understand the effects and risks of cigarettes and alcohol.

CURRICULUM LINKS
QCA science: Unit 5a – Keeping healthy.
KS2: En1 Speaking and listening (3) Group discussion and interaction.

What you need
A 'speaking object' (see the introduction on page 6); photocopiable page 71.

What to do

Introductory phase
● Call out different criteria that relate to keeping healthy, for example: eating fruit; cleaning teeth; and drinking water. Explain that the children who have done these actions during the day may change places in the circle.
● Ask the children to think about one healthy action they have done. Pass the 'speaking object' around the circle and encourage the children to finish the sentence, *One healthy thing I have done today is… .*

Middle phase
● Explain that the lesson is about drugs. Remind the children of the definition of drugs: 'Drugs are substances that affect how a person thinks, feels or behaves'.
● Say that this lesson is about drugs that adults over the age of 16 or 18 can buy and use legally (cigarettes – 16 and alcohol – 18).
● Discuss why it is illegal to sell cigarettes and alcohol to people under the ages of 16 and 18. (Because nicotine found in cigarettes and alcohol have a more damaging effect on younger people and they become addicted more quickly.)
● Ask the children to tell you one thing they know about cigarettes. Pass the 'speaking object' around the circle and encourage the children to finish the sentence, *One thing I know about cigarettes is… .*
● Show the children the sentences on photocopiable page 71 and ask the children to indicate whether they think the statements about alcohol are true or false.

Closing phase
● Explain that smoking and drinking alcohol have risks associated with them. Remind the children that they need to use their knowledge to make sensible choices to keep their bodies healthy.
● The final game involves bodies. Make a simple movement, for example, touch your nose. Ask the next child to copy your movement and add their own. For example, he might touch his nose and then clap his hands.
● The next child repeats the first two actions and adds one of their own. This continues around the circle. No talking is allowed, but others can help with the actions if a child forgets.

Differentiation
Be sensitive to children who may have problem drinkers at home or whose families have religious beliefs that prohibit drinking. Ask older children to tell you at least three things that they know about the affects of alcohol and cigarettes.

AGE RANGE 9–11

LEARNING OBJECTIVE
To know about the effects and risks of drugs and to use basic techniques for resisting pressure to use drugs.

CURRICULUM LINKS
QCA science: Unit 5a – Keeping healthy.
KS2: En1 Speaking and listening (3) Group discussion and interaction (4) Drama.

Saying 'No!'

What you need
A 'speaking object' (see the introduction on page 6).

What to do

Introductory phase
● Think of a four-word sequence concerning substances that we put into or on our bodies, such as: *ointment, apples, cola, shampoo.* Ask the children to repeat the sequence, as fast as possible, in turn, around the circle.
● Now ask the children to think of a sequence using the same criteria. Pass the 'speaking object' around the circle and encourage the children to finish the sentence, *Four things I put on or in my body are… .*

Middle phase
● Remind the children of a simple definition of drugs: *Drugs are substances that affect how a person thinks, feels or behaves.*
● Brainstorm all the drugs that the children can name. If illegal drugs are named, ask the children what effects they think the named illegal drugs have on how a person, thinks, feels or behaves.
● Ask the children what the risks are of putting illegal drugs into their bodies.
● Ensure that the children realise that taking some drugs can be fatal, and that supplying certain drugs can result in imprisonment.
● Discuss why some people start using illegal drugs or why some children try to buy and use alcohol and cigarettes before it is legal.
● Pass the 'speaking object' around the circle and encourage the children to finish the sentence, *I think under-aged children want to try cigarettes or alcohol because… .*
● Tell the children that being assertive and being able to say *No* if they are offered drugs is a skill worth practising.
● Organise the children into pairs. Ask them to role-play a scene where one child acts as persuader, trying to get the other child to try the drugs. The other child takes the part of the child who says *No!*.

Closing phase
● Remind the children that they are responsible for their own bodies and they should identify things that could cause harm to it.
● To end on a happy note ask the children to think of a song that makes them feel happy.
● Pass the 'speaking object' around the circle and encourage the children to tell the circle about their song.

Differentiation
Role-play can be a powerful way for children to practise their response to a risk situation. Allow the children to set the scene for the role-play and tease out useful strategies.

AGE RANGE 5–7

LEARNING OBJECTIVE
To understand rules for, and ways of, keeping safe.

CURRICULUM LINKS
QCA citizenship: Unit 1 – Taking part.
KS1: En1 Speaking and listening (3) Group discussion and interaction.

Safety rules

What you need
A 'speaking object' (see the introduction on page 6); rainstick or music; photocopiable page 72.

What to do

Introductory phase
● Call out instructions for the children to follow, such as: *touch your toes; scratch your nose; jump up and down; clap your hands; and nod your head.* The instructions should get faster and faster and then slow down again.
● Congratulate the children for following the instructions so well. Ask the children to discuss with a partner when or where else they follow instructions.
● Pass the 'speaking object' around the circle and encourage the children to finish the sentence, *I follow instructions when…* .

Middle phase
● Explain that adults often give instructions or rules to keep children safe. Ask if anyone can think of a rule or instruction that helps to keep him or her safe, such as: *Stop, look and listen* when crossing the road.
● Ask the children to think about where safety rules are needed.
● Organise the children into groups of three or four and allocate them a place where safety rules are needed, such as the home, playground, beach, swimming pool and park. Ask each group to decide on the safety rules for their place.
● Ask the groups to report back to the circle.
● Ask the children to think of a place where they feel safe and happy.
● Pass the 'speaking object' around the circle and encourage the children to finish the sentence, *I feel safe and happy…* .

Closing phase
● Congratulate the children for thinking of such good safety rules.
● Ask the children to listen to the rainstick or mood music. Suggest they put their hands on their knees with the palms facing upwards and their fingers slightly curled (this relaxes shoulders and most children find it easy to sit still in this position).
● Ask the children to picture themselves in their safe place. Encourage them to 'look around' and feel safe …
● End the visualisation gently. Bring the children back into the classroom and ask how they are feeling.

Differentiation
Younger or less able children may find it easier to use a copy of photocopiable page 72 in place of the middle phase of the activity. They must circle the risks shown on the picture and then decide on safety rules that apply to it.

 Circle Time

AGE RANGE 6–9

LEARNING OBJECTIVE
To know about trusted people who can help them to stay safe and to judge what kind of physical contact is acceptable or unacceptable.

CURRICULUM LINKS
QCA citizenship: Unit 1 – Taking part; Unit 4 – People who help us.
KS1 and KS2: En1 Speaking and listening (3) Group discussion and interaction.

People we trust

What you need
A 'speaking object' (see the introduction on page 6).

What to do

Introductory phase
● Whisper each child's name in turn. When each name is whispered the child must smile at you and the rest of the circle.
● Pass the speaking object around the circle and encourage the children to finish the sentence, *I whisper when… .*

Middle phase
● Explain that sometimes, secrets are whispered. Ask the children if they have ever had a secret. If so, can they now tell it to the circle?
● Ask the children if anyone can think of a time when it would not be a good idea to keep a secret.
● Stress that any secret that makes the children feel uncomfortable should not be kept.

For example, if another person tries to touch them in a way they do not like; or asks them to touch them in a way the children do not like – they must tell a trusted adult.
● Discuss the qualities of a trusted adult or friend, such as someone you feel safe with or someone who cares about you.
● Organise the children into pairs and ask them to talk about the people they trust.
● Ask the pairs to report back to the circle.
● Discuss the people who the children feel they can trust, from family or friends, to workers in the school or the community (such as police officers). Stress that each child should have a mental list of people they trust who they can turn to for help. It is important that children also know that it is all right to tell a trusted adult about a friend or member of family that has behaved inappropriately towards them.
● Discuss what sort of help they may need from their trusted adult and the reason for choosing which adult to go to for help.

Closing phase
● Ask the children to hold out one hand and to try and name silently one person they can trust for each finger (each child will have five trusted people).
● Finish with a smile – smile at the child on your right or left who then smiles at the next child, and so on around the circle until all the children are smiling. Encourage the children to remember eye-contact when smiling.

Differentiation
Be sensitive to children's circumstances. Use appropriate stories to talk about trustworthy people. The charity Kidscape (www.kidscape.org.uk) offers excellent advice on talking through these difficult issues.

Circle Time

Risky situations

AGE RANGE 6–9

LEARNING OBJECTIVE
To recognise the different risks in different situations and then decide how to behave responsibly.

CURRICULUM LINKS
QCA citizenship: Unit 1 – Taking part; Unit 4 – People who help us.
KS1 and KS2: En1 Speaking and listening (3) Group discussion and interaction.

What you need

A 'speaking object' (see the introduction on page 6); photocopiable page 73 copied onto card and cut into 'scenarios'.

What to do

Introductory phase

● Tell the children that you have placed an imaginary box in the middle of the circle. Ask the children to go up to the box in turn and take out an object and demonstrate its use. The rest of the circle must guess what the object is.

● Pass the 'speaking object' around the circle and encourage the children to finish the sentence, *A dangerous object to have in the box would be... .*

Middle phase

● Explain that the lesson is about recognising risks and behaving so that the children stay safe and well.

● Organise the children into groups of three or four. Using the risk situation cards (cut out from photocopiable page 73) or situations relevant to your school, ask the children to act out the situations and show how they would behave.

● Ask the circle to discuss whether their behaviour was a safe or a dangerous response to the situation.

● Organise the children into pairs to discuss what they do to keep safe. For example: they don't go out in the sun without a hat and cream on; they don't go off with strangers; they wear helmets when cycling, and so on.

● Ask some of the pairs to report back to the circle.

Closing phase

● Remind the children that it is important for them to recognise risks in different situations, and to behave in a way that keeps them safe.

● Explain that the children need to be observant so that they spot a risky situation and the final game reinforces the children's observational skills.

● Ask one child to leave the room. Point to two other children who must change places in the circle. The chosen child returns and has to guess who has changed seats. Repeat the game several times, with different children taking turns.

Differentiation

The age and ability of the children will determine the 'scenarios' used.

How risky?

AGE RANGE 7–11

LEARNING OBJECTIVE
To recognise the different risks in different situations and then decide how to behave responsibly.

CURRICULUM LINKS
QCA citizenship: Unit 1 – Taking part.
KS2: En1 Speaking and listening (3) Group discussion and interaction.

What you need
A 'speaking object' (see the introduction on page 6).

What to do

Introductory phase
● Pretend to pass various risky or dangerous things around the circle, such as: a bottle of medicine; a knife; a pan with hot water in it; a hot iron.
● Pass the 'speaking object' around the circle and encourage the children to finish the sentence, *The most dangerous thing we passed around the circle was… .*

Middle phase
● Thank the children for their answers.
● Explain that the lesson is about deciding how risky situations are.
● Organise the children into pairs to discuss the places in the local community where the most dangerous risks occur, such as roads, beaches, parks, railway lines and so on.
● Divide the children into small groups and ask them to discuss which places they think are the most dangerous and why.
● Ask the groups to report back to the circle, with their thoughts on the most dangerous places and the risks involved.
● Using some local scenarios or the ones below, ask the children to decide, on a sliding scale of one to five (five being high risk), how dangerous the situation could be. Examples include: smoking; playing with matches; riding a bike without a helmet; getting into a car with a woman who is a stranger; getting into a car with a man who is a stranger; eating or drinking an unknown substance.
● Read out each scenario in turn and after each example discuss with the children why they answered the way they did.

Closing phase
● Remind the children that it is important to recognise risks in different situations and to behave in a way that keeps them safe. Tell them that they have an increasing responsibility for their own bodies and behaviour.
● Finish with the following game to lighten the atmosphere. Explain that you have a pretend pot of green 'Gloop' and it's really yucky! You start by throwing the 'Gloop' onto your own face. Pull off the imaginary 'Gloop', making noises and distorting your face! Now throw the 'Gloop' onto the face of a child in the circle – who then repeats the performance of removing the 'Gloop'!
● This continues until everyone in the circle has had a turn.

Differentiation
The age and ability of the children will determine the scenarios used.

Circle Time

Pressure

AGE RANGE 7–11

LEARNING OBJECTIVES
To know that pressure to behave in an unacceptable or risky way can come from a variety of sources, including from people they know; to learn how to ask for help and how to use basic techniques for resisting pressure to do wrong.

CURRICULUM LINKS
QCA citizenship: Unit 1 – Taking part.
KS2: En1 Speaking and listening (3) Group discussion and interaction (4) Drama.

What you need

A 'speaking object' (see the introduction on page 6); a selection of well-known adverts with their product names cut out.

What to do

Introductory phase

● Show the children the adverts with the product names cut out and ask them to guess what the advert is for.
● Ask the children what their favourite advert is, either on the television or in publications. Pass the speaking object around the circle and encourage the children to finish the sentence, *My favourite advert is… .*

Middle phase

● Explain that pressure to buy things is one sort of pressure. Discuss other pressures the children know about. The pressures may have negative or positive outcomes.
● Organise the children in pairs to discuss what sort of pressures their families and friends put them under.
● Ask the pairs to report back to the circle.
● Ask the children to consider whether they ever put pressure on their friends.
● Discuss how it makes the children feel if they are pressurised to do something that makes them feel uncomfortable.
● Explore what the children can do if they feel under pressure. One idea is to be assertive and say *No!.*
● Give the circle practice of saying *No!* in an assertive way. After a count of one, two, three… all the children say *No!.*
● Ask the children to think of pressures they should say *No!* to, such as accepting a cigarette from somebody.
● Ask for volunteers to role-play the situation. The children should take it in turns to be the 'persuader' and the 'resister'. Point out the body language of saying *No!* assertively.

Closing phase

● Emphasise to the children that they should never do something that makes them feel uncomfortable.
● Call out sentences that group the children in different ways. For example, *Whoever likes football come into the middle of the circle and jump up and down; Whoever likes chocolate come into the middle of the circle and smile at everyone.*
● Make a final statement that includes everyone, such as: *Whoever is in my class come to the middle of the circle and shout* 'We are!'.

Differentiation

The age and ability of the children will determine the outcome of the session. Younger children should begin to recognise unwanted influence and pressure whilst older and more mature children should be able to use appropriate strategies to resist pressure, including subtle pressure from friends.

Resisting pressure

AGE RANGE 9–11

LEARNING OBJECTIVE
To know that pressure to behave in an unacceptable or risky way can come from a variety of sources, including from people they know; to learn how to ask for help and how to use basic techniques for resisting pressure to do wrong.

CURRICULUM LINKS
QCA citizenship: Unit 1 – Taking part.
KS2: En1 Speaking and listening (3) Group discussion and interaction (4) Drama.

What you need
A 'speaking object' (see the introduction on page 6); relaxing music.

What to do
Introductory phase
● Organise the children into pairs. Tell the children that you would like them to decide on something that they are going to persuade the class to buy or do. For example, *Buy my lovely red apples they are so good for your health*; or *If you like having fun – join my health club*.
● Pass the 'speaking object' around the circle and encourage the children to put pressure on the rest of the circle to 'buy or do'.

Middle phase
● Explain that the lesson is all about pressure. Tell them that this part of the lesson is not about pressure to buy or go to things, but about pressure to behave in an unacceptable or risky way.
● Organise the children into groups of three or four to discuss pressure to behave in an unacceptable or risky way. What might the pressure be about (smoking, taking drugs, shoplifting, bunking off school)? Who might be doing the persuading?
● Ask the groups to report back to the circle.
● In the same groups, ask the children to develop a role-play using one of the pressures on the list. They should work out an ending where the pressure to behave in an unacceptable or risky way is combated.
● Ask the groups to show their role-plays to the circle.
● At the end of each role-play discuss the effectiveness of each strategy for combating unwanted pressure.

Closing phase
● Congratulate the children for their inventive role-plays and for thinking of ways to resist pressure to do wrong.
● The final activity will allow the children time to reflect upon the role-plays and to relax.
● Play a suitable piece of music that will allow the circle to relax. Ask the children to sit comfortably, close their eyes and listen to the music.

Differentiation
Role-play is an excellent strategy for allowing children to rehearse how they will behave in a difficult situation. The children's suggestions about pressures they know about will enable you to determine where there are issues of concern specific to your class.

Health and safety

AGE RANGE 5–11

LEARNING OBJECTIVE
To know the school rules about health and safety and basic emergency aid procedures.

CURRICULUM LINKS
QCA citizenship: Unit 1 – Taking part.
KS1and KS2: En1 Speaking and listening (3) Group discussion and interaction (4) Drama.

What you need
A 'speaking object' (see the introduction on page 6); a tambourine or bunch of keys.

What to do

Introductory phase
● Explain that you are going to start a story that is added to by the circle. The story is set in the school. Each child should add a minimum of one word or a maximum of a sentence. Tell the children that you will end the story. Congratulate the class for listening to each other.
● Pass the 'speaking object' around the circle and encourage the children to finish the sentence, *I like being in our school because…* .

Middle phase
● Discuss the school rules that ensure your school is a healthy and safe place.
● Explain that sometimes even when rules are in place, accidents and emergencies happen. Ask if anyone can think of an example and how an accident in school was dealt with?
● Explain that emergencies and accidents can happen out of school and it is important to know what to do to help the situation. Stress that it is important that the children keep themselves safe and get help. Very rarely they may have to be the person that contacts the police, fire or ambulance services by dialling 999.
● Explain to the children how to make a 999 call. No money is needed. An operator asks which service you need – police, ambulance or fire brigade. You will then be put through to the service that you require. Tell them that they would need to be ready with some answers (the number of the phone they are using; what has happened and where). They would need to stay calm and speak clearly and slowly.
● Organise the children into groups of two or three so they can practise a scenario of having to dial 999.
● Ask some of the groups to show their role-play to the circle.
● Congratulate the children who behaved appropriately in the scenarios.

Closing phase
● Remind the children that they should only dial 999 if there is an emergency and that all calls are recorded.
● Explain that the session is going to finish in silence. Give the children the tambourine or the large bunch of keys to try to pass around the circle without making a noise.

Differentiation
Teach the lesson in two parts with younger children. They may also need help in deciding which emergency situations require them to dial 999.

We are what we eat

● What should we eat for a healthy dinner?

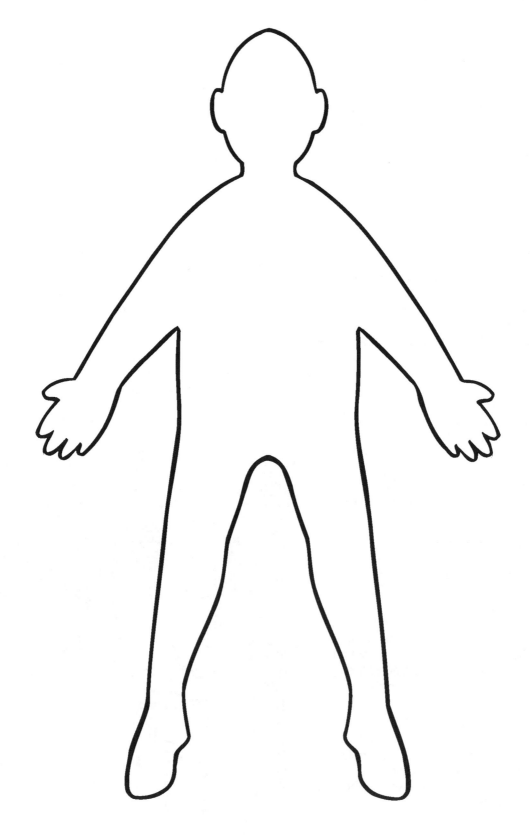

Circle Time **BRIGHT IDEAS**

Healthy choices

- Draw a healthy meal on the plate.
- Divide the plate into sections to show quantities of different types of food.

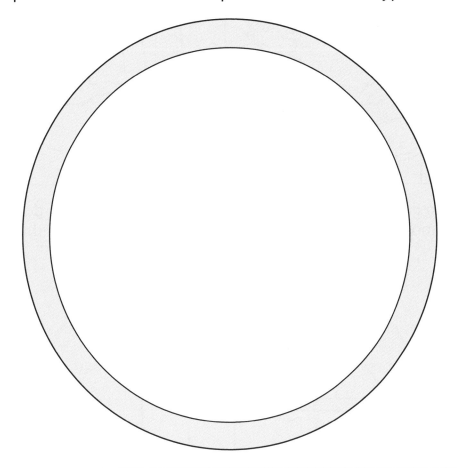

What I should do to keep healthy	What I actually do to keep healthy

Keeping clean

Things I do to get ready in the morning.

Things I do to get ready in the morning.

Things I do to get ready in the morning.

Things I do to get ready for bed.

Things I do to get ready for bed.

Things I do to get ready for bed.

Cigarettes and alcohol

● Are these statements true or false? Circle the word 'True' or 'False' for each one.

1. Anyone can buy alcohol.

    True   False

2. Alcohol can affect peoples' physical and mental state.

    True   False

3. In the UK, 1000 young people are admitted to hospital each week with alcohol poisoning.

    True   False

4. People have known how to make alcohol only for the last 50 years.

    True   False

5. Long-term overuse or abuse of alcohol can lead to damage of the liver, heart and stomach.

    True   False

6. It is safe to drink and drive.

    True   False

Answers
1.False – it is illegal to sell alcohol to anyone under the age of 18. 2. True – alcohol is a depressant and slows the body down. 3. True – some may be unconscious, some vomiting. 4. False – alcohol has been around for hundreds of years. 5. True – alcohol is a drug that does not occur naturally in the human body, so the body can be damaged by too much of it in the system. 6. False – alcohol slows down people's responses. It makes them less able to appreciate danger or respond quickly.

Safety rules

● Circle the risks that you can see in this picture.

Risky situations

● What would you do?

CHAPTER 4

Developing good relationships

Me happy, you happy

AGE RANGE 5–9

LEARNING OBJECTIVE
To recognise that their behaviour affects other people.

CURRICULUM LINKS
QCA citizenship: Unit 1 – Taking part.
KS1 and KS2: En1 Speaking and listening
(3) Group discussion and interaction.

What you need
A 'speaking object' (see the introduction on page 6); a rainstick or suitable music; photocopiable page 90.

What to do

Introductory phase
● Explain to the children that you are 'The Keeper'. Ask the children to chant: *Keeper, Keeper, may we cross your golden lake?* The Keeper replies: *Only if you are…* (use positive attributes such as kind, friendly, helpful, gentle).
● The children who think they have the attribute may cross the circle and change seats with children on the other side who have the same attribute.
● Repeat this game to focus the children on their positive attributes.
● Pass the speaking object around the circle and encourage the children to finish the sentence, *I was kind … .*

Middle phase
● Ask the children to discuss with a partner the sort of kind things that people do. Ask them to talk about how they feel when others are kind to them.
● Explore the idea that we can make others feel sad or cross; frightened or happy. Use characters from appropriate stories to illustrate the point, such as the Fairy Godmother in 'Cinderella' or the Giant in 'Jack and the Beanstalk'.
● Ask the children to discuss with a partner if they ever made someone else feel sad or cross.
● Ask if anyone wants to share an example with the circle.
● You may need to deal with some of the issues raised by this activity. How did it make the children feel when their behaviour made someone else sad or cross. Have they tried not to repeat the hurtful behaviour?

Closing phase
● Encourage the children to thank others in the circle who have been kind to them and have made them feel happy. Congratulate the named children.
● Ask the children to close their eyes and put their hands on their knees with their palms facing upwards and their fingers slightly curled. (This relaxes the children's shoulders and they may find it easier to sit still.)
● Play some music or use the rainstick and encourage the children to listen. Ask them to picture themselves behaving in a way that is making other people feel happy. They will then feel happy and warm inside as well.

Differentiation
Use appropriate literature to explore how words and actions can affect others. Use photocopiable page 90 with younger or less able children to help them consider how the children's behaviour is affecting others.

AGE RANGE 5–9

LEARNING OBJECTIVES
To realise that their actions affect themselves and others; to care about other people's feelings, and to try and see things from another point of view.

CURRICULUM LINKS
QCA citizenship: Unit 1 – Taking part.
KS1 and KS2: En1 Speaking and listening (3) Group discussion and interaction (4) Drama.

Actions and words

What you need
A 'speaking object' (see the introduction on page 6).

What to do

Introductory phase
● Ask the children to stand, then call out different types of shoe (such as walking shoes, ballet shoes, football boots, high-heeled shoes or tap shoes) and ask the children to perform the actions associated with them.
● Ask the children which pair of shoes they would rather wear. Pass the 'speaking object' around the circle and encourage the children to finish the sentence, *I would like to wear… .*

Middle phase
● Explain that you want the children to imagine being in somebody else's shoes, and how the actions and words of others may affect you.
● Organise the children into threes or fours to discuss times when they were made to feel embarrassed, unhappy or angry by others. Then ask them to consider when *their* action may have affected other people. Stress that no names are to be mentioned.
● Ask the groups to return to the circle.
● In the same groups, the children prepare a scenario to show the circle how words and actions can affect others. The scenarios should have two different endings; one with a happy ending and one ending in conflict or unhappiness. The scenarios could be:
  ● Friends playing together when one accidentally hurts one of the others
  ● One friend being teased by a group of others
  ● Friends playing when one kicks the other's ball over the fence
  ● In a shop where one of the group wants to steal something
  ● Playing with a new toy when one of the group breaks it.
● Encourage all the children to do role-play. It's a good way to act out real-life situations in a safe environment.
● Together, explore how things that were said or done in the scenarios affected the outcomes.

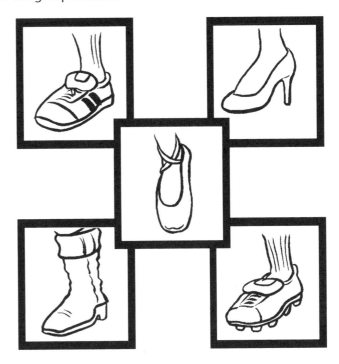

Closing phase
● Encourage the children to thank others in the circle who are good at creating happy endings and thinking about others.
● Ask the children to think of an appropriate gift they would like to give to the child sitting on their right.
● Pass the 'speaking object' around the circle and ask the children to finish the sentence, *My gift to… is… .*

Differentiation
Chose an appropriate scenario that the children can relate to, according to their age group.

Playing together

AGE RANGE 5–7

LEARNING OBJECTIVES
To listen to other people, and to play and work co-operatively.

CURRICULUM LINKS
QCA citizenship: Unit 1 – Taking part.
KS1: En1 Speaking and listening (3) Group discussion and interaction.

What you need
A 'speaking object' (see the introduction on page 6).

What to do

Introductory phase
● Call out instructions that tell the children how to move: *play* means walk forward; *fast forward* means run on the spot; *slow motion* means walk slowly; *stop* ends the game.
● Congratulate the class for listening so well to the instructions, and ask them to think of other games that require them to listen.
● Pass the speaking object around the circle and encourage the children to finish the sentence, *I have to listen when I play…* .

Middle phase
● Put the children into pairs and ask them to discuss games they play where they have to share or take turns.
● Ask the pairs to report their ideas back to the circle.
● Explain that the children often have to cooperate when playing games. Ask if any one knows what 'cooperate' means (to work together as a pair, group, class or team).
● Explain that the next two games require the class to cooperate.
● Tell the children that you are going to start a story that is added to by the circle. Each child adds a minimum of one word or a maximum of a sentence. The teacher ends the story.
● Congratulate the class for listening to each other.
● Perform a 'Mexican wave'. Ask the children to place their hands on their knees. Start the wave by lifting your arms in the air and then back onto your knees, the next person in the circle copies your action, and so on in quick succession.

Closing phase
● Ask the children if there is anyone they would like to thank in the circle for cooperating and sharing and taking turns. Congratulate the named children.
● The final game needs the whole class to cooperate.
● Play 'Pass a gentle squeeze'. Gently squeeze the hand of a child on one side of you. The child squeezes the hand of the child next to them until the squeeze comes back to you. With practise, this can be done so that nobody knows where the squeeze is, until it gets back to the initiator.

Differentiation
If the children find it difficult to cooperate, play more games that will enable them to practise – such as a simple version of 'Touch down' (see the activity 'How others feel' on page 77).

Circle Time

AGE RANGE 7–11

LEARNING OBJECTIVE
To work together and co-operate.

CURRICULUM LINKS
QCA citizenship: Unit 1 – Taking part.
KS2: En1 Speaking and listening (3) Group discussion and interaction.

How others feel

What you need
A 'speaking object' (see the introduction on page 6); a box of items for a guessing game, such as a pencil, book, rubber, sweet and soap.

What to do

Introductory phase
● Place the box of objects in the middle of the circle and choose a volunteer to take something from it (without letting the rest of the class see it).
● The rest of the circle must try to guess what the article is by asking questions. Only 'Yes' or 'No' can be given as answers.
● Explain that it is sometimes difficult to identify items, and even more difficult to identify what others are feeling. We need to know what to listen and look for.
● Ask the children to think of a feeling that they can identify in others and why.
● Pass the 'speaking object' around the circle and encourage the children to finish the sentence, *I can identify… because… .*

Middle phase
● Congratulate the children for being able to identify how others are feeling.
● Put the children into pairs. The game is called 'Touch down'. Explain that when you call a number, each pair must touch the floor with that number of points between them. They can use feet, hands, knees, elbows, and heads as points (so one point is a hand or a foot).
● To play the game the children will need to cooperate with each other. (Define 'cooperate' if necessary.)
● Discuss how the children feel if others will not cooperate with them and why it is easier to cooperate with some children than it is with others.

Closing phase
● Ask the children if there is anyone they would like to thank in the circle for cooperating. Congratulate the named children.
● The final game needs the whole class to think of others and to cooperate.
● Ask one child to stand up and take a statue pose in the middle of the circle. The child sitting on his or her right joins in. Continue around the circle until everyone is part of the statue.

Differentiation
If the children find it difficult to cooperate, play more games that will enable them to practise, such as a 'Mexican wave' (see the activity 'Playing together' on page 76). Restrict 'the points' in the game to hands and feet for younger or less able children.

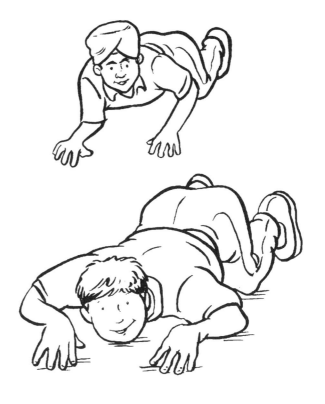

Listen and cooperate

AGE RANGE 6–9

LEARNING OBJECTIVES
To listen to other people, and to play and work cooperatively.

CURRICULUM LINKS
QCA citizenship: Unit 1 – Taking part.
KS1 and KS2: En1 Speaking and listening (3) Group discussion and interaction (4) Drama.

What you need
A 'speaking object' (see the introduction on page 6); photocopiable page 91.

What to do

Introductory phase
● Whisper a sentence to an adjacent child. The sentence must then be passed around the circle in a whisper. When the sentence returns to you, say the received and the original version and compare them.
● Pass the 'speaking object' around the circle and encourage the children to finish the sentence, *I like to listen to… .*

Middle phase
● Discuss why it is important to listen to others.
● Organise the class into groups of three or four. Each group has to think of a job that they can act out (using mime only) for the rest of the class to guess.
● After a few minutes ask the groups to come back into the circle and mime their occupation. The other children try to guess the jobs.
● Establish that to complete the task the children had to cooperate with the rest of the group.
● Discuss what made it hard to cooperate.
● In the same groups, let the children discuss why is it important to cooperate with others.

Closing phase
● Ask the children to thank others who cooperate in work and play. Congratulate the named children.
● Explain that the final game needs the circle to cooperate to help other class members find a hidden object. Ask one child to go outside the room; hide a small object.
● The child outside comes back in and has to find the object. The class help by clapping louder when the seeker is close to the object. When they are far away the clapping is very soft.

Differentiation
Focus less-able children on the concept of cooperation by asking them to complete photocopiable page 91 in pairs or small groups. Emphasise that they need to work together and invite each child to draw a part of the picture. If the children require further experience of cooperating, use other lessons to develop their skills. For example, in PE – play team games or aim to achieve a group task (such as several children lifting a PE mat into place or helping each other to put out the apparatus).

Circle Time **BRIGHT IDEAS**

AGE RANGE 5–7

LEARNING OBJECTIVE
To identify and respect the differences and similarities between people.

CURRICULUM LINKS
QCA citizenship: Unit 1 – Taking part; Unit 5 – Living in a diverse world.
KS1: En1 Speaking and listening (3) Group discussion and interaction.

Similarities and differences

What you need
A 'speaking object' (see the introduction on page 6); photocopiable page 92, showing children from different cultures; music from different cultures; a beanbag.

What to do

Introductory phase
● Play some music from different cultures. Explain that when the music starts, the children must dance around the circle. When the music stops – the children freeze. Any child who moves is out and sits down for one turn before rejoining the game.
● Pass the 'speaking object' around the circle and encourage the children to finish the sentence, *My favourite music/song is… .*

Middle phase
● Give out copies of photocopiable page 92 and discuss the children in the pictures. Talk about what the children in your class have in common with them, then begin to note the differences.
● Next, ask the children to look at each other and spot similarities and differences.
● Give one child a beanbag and ask him to name a child he has something in common with, then throw the beanbag to him or her. For example, *I have brown eyes and so does Joe.* Joe then chooses something he has in common with someone else. For example, *I am wearing a red sweatshirt and so is Ellie.*
● Ask the children to ensure that everyone in the circle is included.

Closing phase
● Explain that all of the children are special and unique and that they all need to be treated with kindness and consideration. Ask the children to thank others who do that.
● Now invite everyone to stand up and hold hands. Swing arms and chant: *We are special!* On the word 'special', everyone (still holding hands) raises their arms above their heads. Arms are lowered and the chant is repeated.

Differentiation
Any activity that focuses on the way that people look needs to be treated with sensitivity. Make sure that all the children feel included in the discussion and offer support to less able children by asking questions to guide their responses. For example, *Can you tell me something about the clothes that the children are wearing?*. Challenge older or more able children to think of similarities and differences that are not as visible as the ones discussed in the lesson.

AGE RANGE 5–11

LEARNING OBJECTIVES
To identify and respect the differences and similarities
between people; to think about the lives of people with
different values and customs.

CURRICULUM LINKS
QCA citizenship: Unit 1 – Taking part; Unit 5 – Living in a
diverse world.
KS1 and KS2: En1 Speaking and listening (3) Group
discussion and interaction.

Celebrations

What you need
A 'speaking object' (see the
introduction on page 6);
music from different cultures;
photocopiable page 93.

What to do

Introductory phase
● Remove one chair from the
circle and play a few rounds of
'Musical chairs'. The children
must move around the circle
to music, and when the music
stops they need to find a chair.
The person left without a chair
is out. The game continues
until just one child is left in.

● Explain that 'Musical chairs'
is often played at parties or
celebrations. Ask the children
which other party games they like to play.
● Pass the 'speaking object' around the circle and encourage the children to finish the
sentence, *A party game I like to play is… .*

Middle phase
● Explain that because we are all different we often celebrate occasions and events in
different ways.
● Ask the children to work with a partner. Invite them to tell each other about
celebrations they have at home. Encourage them to talk about their traditions
surrounding the celebration.
● Ask the pairs to report their ideas to the circle.
● Using photocopiable page 93 and the children's experiences, explore the similarities
and differences that make up the celebrations.
● Pass the 'speaking object' around the circle and encourage the children to finish the
sentence, *My favourite celebration is… .*

Closing phase
● Thank the children for sharing the different ways they celebrate.
● Explain that all of the children are special and unique and that they all need to be
treated with kindness and consideration. Ask the children to thank others who do that.
● Invite the children to decide on a favourite game that they like to play at a
celebration. If there is a consensus and you are clear about the rules, then play it
together.
● Alternatively, another game is to ask the children to stand up. Establish eye-contact
and smile at a child, then sit down. The smiled-at child then smiles at another child
before sitting down. Continue until all the children are sitting down.

Differentiation
Delve deeper into the traditions of various festivals and celebrations. Use photocopiable
page 93 with younger children and share some non-fiction books together. Set
challenges for older children, such as asking them to undertake some guided internet
research.

Families and friends

AGE RANGE 5–11

LEARNING OBJECTIVE
To be aware of different types of relationships between friends and families, and to develop skills to be effective in relationships.

CURRICULUM LINKS
QCA citizenship: Unit 1 – Taking part.
KS1 and KS2: En1 Speaking and listening (3) Group discussion and interaction.

What you need
A 'speaking object' (see the introduction on page 6).

What to do

Introductory phase
● Call out a four-word sequence, such as *Mum, Dad, Brother, Sister*. The children in turn say the next word in the sequence (Mum, Dad, Brother or Sister) around the circle.
● The game should be played as fast as possible. When the sequence has been around the circle once, ask one of the children to introduce a new sequence involving family members.
● Now ask the children to think of a family member or a friend who is special to them. Encourage them to think of a reason as to why they are special.
● Pass the speaking object around the circle and encourage the children to finish the sentence, *[chosen person] is special because… .*

Middle phase
● Discuss the idea that we can't choose our family members – but we can choose our friends (who may also be members of our families).
● Ask the children to work with one or two people they don't know very well and tell them what they like to do with their friends.
● In their groups, ask the children to discuss what makes a good friend.
● Ask the groups to report back to the circle.
● Invite the children to think about and reflect upon what makes *them* a good friend. Ask if anyone will share his or her thoughts with the circle.

Closing phase
● Ask the children to thank others in the circle for being a good friend.
● Suggest to the children that if they notice anyone who is having trouble making friends, they might like to help them by offering advice and support. One of the ways they can do this is to use a 'script', such as: *Would it help if I/you/we…?.*
● Explain that the final game involves asking questions. Tell the children that you are thinking about one of the children in the circle. The children take turns to question you, to try to guess the child you are thinking about. You may only answer *Yes* or *No.*

Differentiation
Suggest that younger children think more about a particular friend. Encourage older children to think about a group of friends – they could look at what they like to do as a group and how they are good friends to each other.

AGE RANGE 7–11

LEARNING OBJECTIVE
To develop skills to be effective in relationships.

CURRICULUM LINKS
QCA citizenship: Unit 1 – Taking part.
KS2: En1 Speaking and listening (3) Group discussion and interaction. (3d) To deal politely with different points of view.

Friendship

What you need
A 'speaking object' (see the introduction on page 6); paper and pencils.

What to do

Introductory phase
● Choose a child to be 'a caller' who stands in the middle of the circle. The children stand up and the caller says either: *All move left* or *All move right*. The children move along to their new chair and sit down.
● When the caller says, *All change*, every child changes seats with another child. The caller tries to find herself a seat so that there is a new caller in the middle of the circle.
● When the children are confident with this game, the caller can say move any number of chairs to the right or the left. The children are now mixed up in the circle.
● Pass the 'speaking object' around the circle and encourage the children to finish the sentence, *I like to sit near my friend because…* .

Middle phase
● Explain that the lesson is about friendship. Ask the children to form groups of two or three with their friends.
● Now invite the children to discuss what makes a good friend. They need to decide upon what they think are the three most important qualities (kindness, thoughtfulness, loyalty, honesty, caring and so on). The children write their chosen three most important qualities on the paper provided.
● Organise the groups so that they join with another group. Challenge the combined groups to decide which of the qualities they have on their papers are the three most important. This requires the children to negotiate and reach a consensus.
● Collect the ideas from all the groups and put their papers in the middle of the circle.
● Explore the different qualities that they have chosen and ask the children to nominate the one most important to them.

Closing phase
● Ask the children to thank others in the circle for possessing any of the named qualities.
● Ask one child to leave the room. Ask three or four children to make positive statements about him. When the child returns, he stands in the middle of the circle, and the teacher repeats the statements. The child has to guess who said what about him.

Differentiation
Younger or less able children may need support to record their ideas. Invite younger children to draw pictures of the people who are their friends. Invite older children to make a mind-map about what makes a good friend.

Circle Time BRIGHT IDEAS

AGE RANGE 7–11

LEARNING OBJECTIVE
To be aware of different types of relationships and to
develop skills to be effective in relationships.

CURRICULUM LINKS
QCA citizenship: Unit 1 – Taking part.
KS2: En1 Speaking and listening (3) Group discussion
and interaction. (3d) To deal politely with different
points of view.

Relationships

What you need
A 'speaking object' (see the
introduction on page 6);
photocopiable page 94.

What to do

Introductory phase
● Begin a sentence: *I went to
the zoo and saw an elephant... .*
The next child repeats and adds
another animal: *I went to the zoo
and saw an elephant and a tiger... .*
● Continue around the circle
until someone repeats an animal
or cannot think of a new animal.
That person begins a new
sentence. For example: *I went to
the shop and bought...*
● Ask the pupils to think of a
place they go to with their friends.
Pass the 'speaking object' around
the circle and encourage the
children to finish the sentence,
With my friend/friends I go to... .

Middle phase
● Explain that the lesson is about relationships and how to make and keep friends.
● Organise the children into groups of three or four and ask them to discuss why
friends sometimes fall out and what can be done to make-up again.
● The groups report back to the circle.
● Stress that at times, friends have to compromise. Ask if they can tell you what
'compromise' means.
● Ask the children to think of a time when they compromised or did something for
their friend or friends.
● Pass the 'speaking object' around the circle and encourage the children to finish the
sentence, *I was a good friend when I... .*

Closing phase
● Ask the children if there is anyone in the circle who has been a good friend to them
or if they have noticed someone in the circle being a good friend to someone else.
● Finish with a fun observation game. Ask one child to leave the room. Point to two
other pupils who change places in the circle. The chosen child returns and has 30
seconds to guess who has changed seats.

Differentiation
Use photocopiable page 94 with younger children. Ask them to fill in the concentric
circles with pictures of those they are close to or acquainted with. Their face should fill
the centre circle, with those closest to them depicted in the nearest touching circle.
Challenge older children to complete the photocopiable page without any help and
then suggest that they go on to design their own network of family and friends.

Developing relationships

AGE RANGE 9–11

LEARNING OBJECTIVE
To be aware of different types of relationships, including marriage and those between friends and families, and to develop skills to be effective in relationships.

CURRICULUM LINKS
QCA citizenship: Unit 1 – Taking part.
KS2: En1 Speaking and listening (3) Group discussion and interaction.

What you need
A 'speaking object' (see the introduction on page 6).

What to do

Introductory phase
● Put a spare chair into the circle. The leader calls a child's name and she moves to the empty chair.
● The child to the left of the empty chair calls the name of a different child across the circle, who then moves to the empty chair. Continue until all the children have had a turn and they are not sitting next to a chosen friend.
● Pass the 'speaking object' around the circle and encourage the children to finish the sentence, *When I can't sit near my friend I feel…* .

Middle phase
● Explain that the lesson is about relationships. With the children, brainstorm a list of the different types of relationships, such as parents, children, siblings, wives, husbands, friends and acquaintances.
● Discuss what makes a good relationship.
● Organise the children into friendship groups of two or three to discuss marriage. Why do some people get married? Why do some people choose not to get married? Why do some people get divorced? (You will need to be very sensitive to the needs and experiences of your class.)
● Ask the groups to report what they have discussed to the circle.
● In the same groups, ask the children to discuss what attributes make a good relationship work (such as kindness, honesty, loyalty, care, thoughtfulness, fun, humour and love).
● Ask the groups to tell the circle about the qualities they chose.
● Organise a vote to find the top five things needed to make a relationship work.

Closing phase
● Ask the children to think of a gift they would like to give to someone that they have a relationship with. For example, they may want to give their mother a holiday, or their best friend a cinema ticket.
● Pass the 'speaking object' around the circle and encourage the children to finish the sentence, *I would give my… a… because…* .

Differentiation
Be sensitive to children's circumstances and only use the part of the lesson about marriage if you feel it is suitable. For younger or less able children, talk about developing good relationships with friends and/or family members.

Circle Time **BRIGHT IDEAS**

AGE RANGE 5–7

LEARNING OBJECTIVE
To realise that bullying is wrong and to discuss how to
deal with bullying.

CURRICULUM LINKS
QCA citizenship: Unit 1 – Taking part
KS1: En1 Speaking and listening (3) Group discussion
and interaction.

Teasing

What you need
A 'speaking object' (see the introduction on page 6); a box containing three things to make a noise, such as a shaker, a bell and scrunched-up paper; a ball of wool.

What to do

Introductory phase
● Introduce the children to the box of noises.
● Tell the children that for each noise you make they must perform a different action. For example: shaker – stand and scratch nose; bell – stand and rub elbow; paper – sit and fold arms.
● Make the noises thick and fast!
● Now ask the children to think about how the game was played and how they would change it.
● Pass the 'speaking object' around the circle and encourage the children to finish the sentence, *My noise and action would be… .*

Middle phase
● Explain that the lesson is about teasing.
● Organise the children into pairs to discuss if they have ever been teased either playfully or hurtfully. How did it make them feel?
● Ask the pairs to report their ideas back to the circle.
● Discuss the difference between teasing and bullying.
● Teasing can be playful and fun but it can become bullying if it is repeated and deliberately hurtful.
● Ask the children to think of ways to stop bullies from repeatedly and deliberately hurting others.
● Pass the 'speaking object' around the circle and encourage the children to finish the sentence, *My idea to stop bullies is… .*

Closing phase
● Thank the children for sharing their wonderful ideas.
● Pass the ball of wool across the circle, keeping hold of the end. The child who receives the wool passes the wool around their waist or wrist and passes the ball across the circle to another child. This continues until all the children are in the 'tangle.' Make sure that the children do not tug on the wool, as this will hurt!
● In silence, the children keep still and think about a safe place, such as their bed, garden or the classroom.
● Finish by trying to untangle!

Differentiation
Set up and take part in some role-play work with younger children to help them to understand the difference between teasing and bullying.

AGE RANGE 7–11

LEARNING OBJECTIVE
To realise the nature of bullying and aggressive
behaviour, and to learn how to respond to these
behaviours and ask for help.

CURRICULUM LINKS
QCA citizenship: Unit 1 – Taking part.
KS2: En1 Speaking and listening (3) Group discussion
and interaction (4) Drama.

It is not funny

What you need
A 'speaking object' (see the introduction on page 6).

What to do

Introductory phase
● Ask the children to move around the circle asking each other questions. The idea is
to trick the other children into answering a question with a *Yes* or a *No*. Ask the children
to keep count of how many times another child says *Yes* or *No* to them.
● After a few minutes count up how many times *Yes* and *No* has been said to each
child.
● Ask the children how they felt when playing the game. Pass the 'speaking object'
around the circle and encourage the children to finish the sentence, *When playing the
game I felt… .*

Middle phase
● Discuss teasing and bullying with the children (including 'put downs' in the
discussion).
● Organise the children into groups to discuss teasing and bullying and how these
actions make the victim feel.
● Explain that being able to respond assertively to bullying means that the children
have less chance of being the victim and more chance of helping a victim. Ask for a
definition of 'assertive' (one definition is being forceful without becoming aggressive).
● Explain that the children are going to be given a chance to practise being assertive.
● Organise the children into threes or fours. They are to role-play a scenario where
one of them is the victim and the others are bullies or bystanders. The victims and
bystanders have to respond to the bullying in an assertive way. Allow time for the
children to change roles.
● Choose one or two of the groups to show their role-play to the circle.
● Pass the 'speaking object' around the circle and encourage the children to finish the
sentence, *If I was a victim I would… .*

Closing phase
● Congratulate the children for their
super ideas.
● Nominate one child to be the
detective – they must leave the room.
● While the detective is out of the
room, a leader is chosen to perform
an action that the rest of the class
must follow. When the leader changes
action the class must continue to
follow.
● The detective comes back into
the room and tries to guess who the
leader is.

Differentiation
Make sure that the role-play scenarios
that you suggest are suited to the
age, ability and experience of the
children in the different groups.

Circle Time

AGE RANGE 7–9

LEARNING OBJECTIVE
To recognise and challenge stereotypes.

CURRICULUM LINKS
QCA citizenship: Unit 1 – Taking part; Unit 5 – Living in a diverse world.
KS2: En1 Speaking and listening (3) Group discussion and interaction (4) Drama.

Stereotypes

What you need
A 'speaking object' (see the introduction on page 6); photocopiable page 95.

What to do

Introductory phase
● Before the lesson ask the children to quickly draw a picture of a footballer and a nurse.
● Ask each child to think of a job that they can mime.
● Ask the children to perform their mime and invite the rest of the circle to guess the job.
● Pass the 'speaking object' around the circle and encourage the children to finish the sentence, *When I leave school I want to be a … .*

Middle phase
● Go around the circle asking the children to show and describe their footballer and nurse pictures.
● Discuss the gender of the drawings and whether there any jobs that only a female or a male can do.
● Explain the word 'stereotyping' and how it can lead to discrimination because people may not be expected to do certain jobs because of their gender.
● Tell the children that you are going to read out some statements and that you want the children to stand up if they disagree with the statement; stay sitting with their arms folded if they agree and sit down with their hands on their heads if they are unsure.
● Make statements such as:
  ● Women are better at housekeeping than men
  ● Men are better car mechanics than women
  ● Women should look after children, whilst men go out to work.
● If there are a variety of opinions about a statement, stop and ask the children that disagree to challenge the children who agree with the statement.

Closing phase
● Congratulate the children for beginning to recognise stereotypes.
● Finish with a funny miming game. Start a mime, such as washing your face. The child on your right asks you, *What are you doing?*. You must not be truthful and instead say something like *I'm milking a cow!*. The child must mime milking a cow and the child on her right asks her, *What are you doing?*. And so the game continues until everyone is involved.

Differentiation
Introduce the concept of stereotyping with photocopiable page 95. Ask the children to guess the jobs of the three (non-stereotypical) people (bus driver, doctor, teacher). Then ask them to draw three pictures of their own to match the words. Compare the results. Invite older children to think about examples where stereotypes have been challenged, for example, female priests.

AGE RANGE 9–11

LEARNING OBJECTIVE
To recognise and challenge stereotypes.

CURRICULUM LINKS
QCA citizenship: Unit 1 – Taking part; Unit 5 – Living
in a diverse world.
KS2: En1 Speaking and listening (3) Group discussion
and interaction.

It's obvious

What you need
A 'speaking object' (see the
introduction on page 6).

What to do
Introductory phase
● Ask for a volunteer to stand in
the middle of the circle. Ask the rest
of the circle to think of one obvious
positive thing about the volunteer.
● The volunteer chooses a child
who must make an obvious
statement, such as, *It's obvious that
you have a pair of trainers*. After
three statements the volunteer in
the middle is changed.
● Ask the children to think about
one thing that is obvious about
themselves.
● Pass the 'speaking object'
around the circle and encourage the
children to finish the sentence, *It's
obvious that I… .*

Middle phase
● Explain that sometimes we think
things are obvious when they are not. Often we use stereotypical information (we might
have a simplified stock image of a person or a nation).
● Use the 'speaking object' to go around the circle asking each child to say a different
nationality. Children near the end of the circle may ask for help.
● Organise the children into groups of three or four and using the nationalities
suggested by the children, ask them to make a statement about them. For example,
the Welsh can all sing well; Brazilians love to party; English people all drink tea.
● Ask the groups to report some of their ideas back to the circle. Are they based on
facts, or are they stereotypes of different nationalities?
● In their groups, ask the children to discuss the country in which they were born and
any facts about the people who live there.
● Ask the groups to report back to the circle.

Closing phase
● Congratulate the children for beginning to recognise stereotypes. They need to be
alert to assumptions based on stereotyping and be ready to challenge them.
● Finish with this 'leaving' game. A volunteer starts the game by saying to the circle,
My name is … and I'm leaving you now with a wave. The next person in the circle says
their name and a different action, such as, *My name is… and I'm leaving you now with a
wink*. Continue until everyone has contributed.

Differentiation
Encourage older or more able children to do some research on selected countries before
the circle time activity. Invite them to challenge some of the stereotypical images of
countries and their people based on their research knowledge.

In common

AGE RANGE 7–11

LEARNING OBJECTIVE
To learn that differences and similarities between people arise from a number of factors, including cultural, ethnic, racial and religious diversity, gender and disability.

CURRICULUM LINKS
QCA citizenship: Unit 1 – Taking part; Unit 5 – Living in a diverse world.
KS2: En1 Speaking and listening (3) Group discussion and interaction.

What you need
A 'speaking object' (see the introduction on page 6); a beanbag.

What to do

Introductory phase
● Call out questions that group the children in different ways. For example, *Whoever likes football come into the middle of the circle and jump up and down,* or *Whoever likes chocolate come into the middle of the circle and smile at everyone.* The final statement should be: *Whoever is in my class come to the middle of the circle and shout, 'We are!'.*
● Pass the speaking object around the circle and encourage the children to finish the sentence, *One thing about me that is the same as everyone else is… .*

Middle phase
● Explain that the lesson is about things the children have in common – similarities and differences.
● Discuss gender differences. Ask if anyone has heard a sexist comment (such as, *Boys can do it better than girls!*).
● Discuss differences that can be seen, such as gender, race and some disabilities.
● Organise the children into groups of three or four and ask them to make up a story about a world where all the people are the same gender and the same colour – they all act in the same way, and no differences are allowed!
● Ask one or two of the groups to report back to the circle and tell their stories. What issues did the stories raise?
● Discuss differences that can't be seen such as likes, dislikes and chosen hobbies.

Closing phase
● Congratulate the children for being able to appreciate the differences between people.
● Give one child a beanbag and ask them to name a child they have something in common with and then throw the beanbag to them. For example, *I like curry and so does Amelia.* Amelia then chooses something that she has in common with someone else. For example, *I have a pet and so does Benjamin.* Ensure that everyone in the circle is included.

Differentiation
Younger children may need to start the story with guidance as a whole circle rather than in small groups. Challenge older children to make up a role-play about what a world without difference would be like.

Me happy, you happy

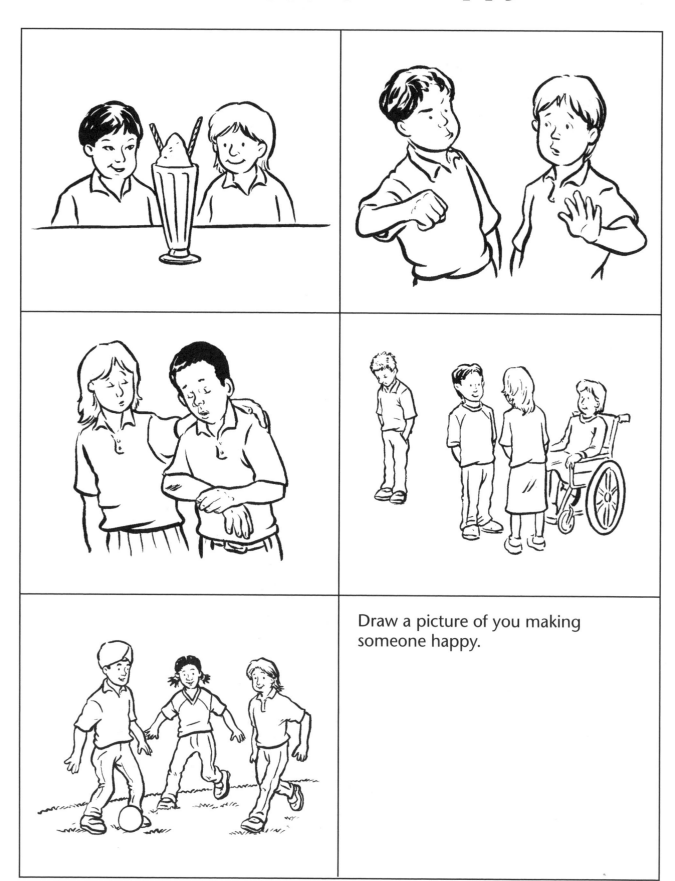

Draw a picture of you making someone happy.

Circle Time **BRIGHT IDEAS**

Listen and cooperate

● Finish drawing the scene below.

Similarities and differences

Circle Time **BRIGHT IDEAS**

Celebrations

Relationships

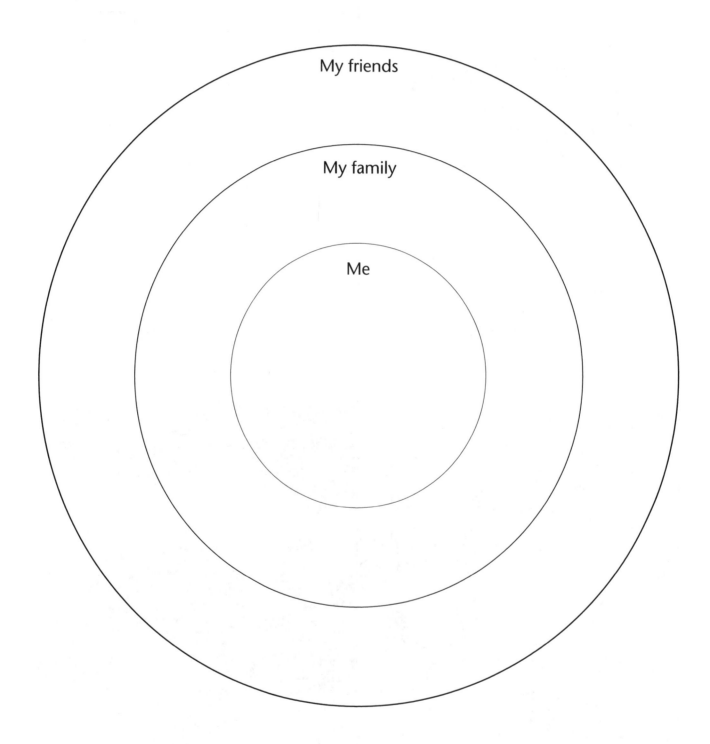

My friends

My family

Me

Stereotypes

● What job do these people do?

Draw a nurse.

Draw a ballet dancer.

Monday 25th May

Where do these animals live?

Owl
Seal
Caterpillar

Draw an engineer.

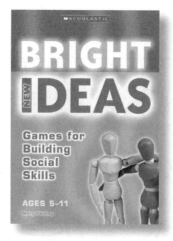